the
INCLUSIVE
MINDSET

the
INCLUSIVE

MINDSET

How to Cultivate **DIVERSITY** in Your **EVERYDAY LIFE**

JUSTIN JONES-FOSU

 Peter
Jones
Publishing

Published in Charlotte, North Carolina, by Peter Jones Publishing

Editor: Darcie Clemen Robertson
Cover design: U.T. Designs
Interior design: Katherine Lloyd, www.thedeskonline.com
Back cover author picture: Ariel Perry
Chapter cartoons: Ricky Castillo

The stories shared throughout this book were gathered through personal interviews with the author, and accuracy has been ensured to the best of the publisher's ability. Permission was obtained for each of the personal stories shared. A few names have been changed to protect the privacy of the persons involved. Any internet addresses, phone numbers, or company or product information printed in this book is offered as a resource and is not intended in any way to be or to imply an endorsement by the publisher, nor does the publisher vouch for the existence, content, or services of these sites, phone numbers, companies, or products beyond the life of this book.

The story of the glass half full in chapter 12 originally appeared in *Your Why Matters Now,* published by Peter Jones Publishing.

ISBN: 978-0-9833718-8-5 Hardcover
          978-0-9833718-7-8 Paperback
          978-0-9833718-9-2 Ebook

Printed in the United States of America
21 22 23 KDP 3 2 1

To my mom-e, who I had no idea was exposing me to so
many different cultures and people while I was growing up.
You are my true diversity and inclusion hero!

⚬⚬⚬⚬⚬⚬

To my amazing kiddos, Lydia and Peter.
You are my "why" behind this work, as I want to
help create a better world for you to inherit.

CONTENTS

THE INCLUSIVE MINDSET VISION

The World Can Be a Place Where . . .

People are treated with value, dignity, and respect no matter what they look like, how they identify, or what they believe.

People engage others every day with a sense of wonderment and curiosity.

People disagree respectfully while honoring the perspectives of others.

Everyone feels included, seen, and heard, and the voices of the marginalized are elevated and amplified.

People stand up for others when they see injustice occurring and challenge systems that don't work for others.

People don't have to be perfect and can receive grace as they learn from their mistakes.

Diversity and inclusion are no longer an initiative but part of our everyday lives, and no longer a mandate but simply a mindset.

This is the world we believe in. This is what we believe *the world can be.*

part one

INTRODUCING
THE INCLUSIVE
MINDSET

Chapter 1

WHAT TYPE
OF HUGGER ARE YOU?

Embracing the Right Approach

grew up in a very hug-filled family. I am a mama's boy, and I constantly hugged my mother when I was a child. When I had a dog and a cat, I gave them endless hugs. I love hugging so much that my kids get at least 15.8 hugs a day from me—well, maybe only 14.7. Some hugs are when we're both standing and other hugs occur when I lift them up, swing them around, and squeeze super tight. I love hugs so much I have even learned to hug myself (don't judge it until you've tried it).

HOW DO YOU HUG?

What type of hugger are you? I realize there are different types of hugs and greetings. There is the formal handshake greeting. There is the "dap." And when you are really cool, your hands glide into an embrace. There is the hand hug (does anyone still do this one?). There is the classic side hug. There is the "I'm not going to let my body touch you" hug. And there is the—wait for it—full-frontal embrace hug. You know, the type of hug where you can feel the ribs of the other person. Some people call this a bear hug, but I call this a normal hug (well, for those I know who allow me to hug them this way). Which one are you?

Did you know that research has confirmed that hugs actually help reduce negative emotions during conflict? Hugs have been proven to improve mood and psychological well-being.[1] There is also research suggesting that when we hug someone, chemicals are produced in our brains that soothe us and make us feel safer, which might even lead to a decrease in depression.[2]

Now, I know some of you are reading this and saying, "Justin, I don't want to hug you, or anyone else for that matter." You might be thinking, *If I have to hug someone, then maybe I will not have an Inclusive Mindset.* Don't put the book down quite yet. This book isn't about hugging (even though that would be a marvelously awesome book). But it is about embracing something, and that something is diversity and inclusion (which over time might lead to an increase in our mood too).

By *diversity* and *inclusion* I mean engaging those who are different from you. Diversity and inclusion have been misinterpreted by many over the years, but the terms simply mean seeing the humanity in others (yes, even those you disagree with) and treating them with value, decency, and respect.

Diversity and inclusion are important because every single one of us is impacted by how diversity and inclusion play out in our daily lives. In some ways we are all different. We all have unique qualities, and everyone deserves to feel seen, heard, and valued.

Unfortunately, we live in a world where we can dehumanize others simply because they disagree with us or because they look different from us. Even with those I vehemently disagree with, I challenge myself (and it is hard at times) to see their humanity and treat them with respect because they are human beings. After all, wouldn't you want others to treat you and those you love with the same decency? I want my kids to grow up in a world that is more decent, respectful, and understanding than the one that currently exists. I want them to grow up in a world where they will be embraced and others can embrace them despite their differences. This book will help you and me do just that by helping all of us to develop an Inclusive Mindset.

An Inclusive Mindset is an echo of the vision I shared at the beginning of the book (go ahead and read it if you skipped it earlier). The Inclusive Mindset is when we approach the world with a sense of wonderment and curiosity. It is when we focus on how we progress and get better no matter where we are starting from. It is where we are less concerned if we get it all right and are more concerned about growing a deeper and more impactful understanding of the world and the human beings within it. The Inclusive Mindset is about noticing how diversity is present in our lives every single day if we acknowledge it and find ways to include more people and move toward having a more beautiful life. When we have this type of thinking, when we feel for others in this type of way, we know we are beginning to embrace diversity and inclusion not just at the head level but at the heart level, which leads to meaningful action and progress.

HOW DO YOU "EMBRACE" DIVERSITY AND INCLUSION?

Some of us approach diversity and inclusion like a formal handshake. We are engaging with it because we feel we must, or because society is shifting, or because our organization has said it is important and might be strongly suggesting that everyone go through some sort of training and development. Some of you are on the other side of the spectrum, and you have fully embraced diversity and inclusion—you know the terms, the acronyms, the research, the movies . . . heck, you might have even changed your middle name to D&I (or DEI if you are all in)! There are a whole lot of you who might be somewhere in between, and I'm writing to share that no matter where you are, you have an opportunity to grow, progress, and develop.

You might even be reading this as a non-hugger, and you don't think it's important to embrace diversity and inclusion at all. In over a decade of doing this work, I have encountered quite a few of you, and my hope is that you would also take the time to read and engage. And when you do, I believe you will see that true diversity and inclusion are valuable after all. While many of you might not get to the end of this book and be full-frontal embracers of diversity and inclusion, my hope is that you would have progressed up the hugging spectrum and that this book and approach will be helpful as you encounter your communities, workplaces, and ultimately the ever-connected world.

HOW I CAME TO EMBRACE DIVERSITY AND INCLUSION

My mother, whom I affectionately call Mom-e, is the culprit. When my brother and I were growing up, there was a season when we did not have the financial ability to go to events (we were cash poor). What I love about her is that she did not let that stop her from exposing my brother and me to many different things, places, and people in Grand Rapids, Michigan. We went to pow-wows, Oktoberfest, and countless cultural festivals (Polish, Russian, German, etc.), and she made me go to community events (did I mention I did not want to go?). When we couldn't afford to go, we did what many families do in that situation . . . we volunteered. I just wanted to go skating, talk to the young ladies, play basketball, talk to the young ladies, play video games, and yep, you guessed it . . . talk to the young ladies, but here was my mom-e making me go to events I did not understand and many times did not even like. Why, oh why, Mom-e, would you do that to me?

I now understand that my passion to be curious, to learn about others, and to engage with things I do not understand or even like came from my first diversity and inclusion hero, my mom-e. She was developing an Inclusive Mindset in me long before I could even articulate the concept to others. My mom-e credits her curiosity to reading. I called her when I was writing this book, and she told me, "I liked to read a lot and considered myself a child of the Universe." When I asked her what inspired her to expose my brother and me to other cultures, she said, "I wanted you all to [experience] other cultures because I thought it was enlightening." She shared that when she was a young military woman in Yokota, Japan, it annoyed her that some of the US soldiers never left the military base. "I wanted to expose you to things so that you wouldn't have the attitude and mindset of those soldiers."[3]

We not only went to events; we invited people into our home. We were host families for international exchange students from Germany, Japan, France, and Brazil (well, the Brazilian young lady lasted one day and asked to be sent to another family when she realized we were a Black family). One of those exchange students, Irene, lived with us for a year, and I still consider her a sister to this day and visit her often.

Who were the people or events in your life that started you on your diversity and inclusion journey? Maybe it was a major event that happened in our society, and maybe for some of you it will be this book, but whatever it is I am glad you are on this journey with me.

MY FULL EMBRACE

Multiple past life experiences have led me to fully embrace diversity and inclusion as a way of life. Not that I always agree with everyone or everything I hear that is "different," but the full embrace is holding an idea long enough to know if I want to hold it again and again. Sometimes one hug is enough, and sometimes I can't stop hugging that difference. I remember the first time I really realized I was different. I was a paperboy skating down the street in East Grand Rapids (which was traditionally a well-to-do white area). This was my paper route, and I was so excited to delight my customers with my amazing paper-tossing abilities. I was singing to myself as I was going down the street when some white guys yelled out of the car and called me the N-word. I had heard that word before, but it had never been directed at me, and I remember thinking to myself, *What did I do to them?* (I am getting a little emotional even as I type this.) I pondered what would cause someone to be so cruel and so mean to a thirteen-year-old paperboy.

I remember we were the only Black family at the church across the street from our house where I was in the choir, rang bells, and lit the candles. I remember growing up in a predominantly Black neighborhood but going to an almost all-white school for the "smart kids." I never felt Black enough for the Black kids, and I never felt white enough for the white kids. I felt like I was on an island.

Fast-forward to the summer of 2004. I was doing an internship and was going through cultural intelligence training. As I sat in the U-shaped classroom and the instructors talked, I had an epiphany and started weeping. I realized that the reason I felt the tension in my all-white church growing up and at my predominantly Black university (shout-out to historically Black colleges and universities: HBCUs) was because I was meant to be a bridge, and it was at that moment I knew I would be part of the solution to help bring different people together.

My mind went back to another internship, this one with Coca-Cola, where fifty of us interns, who lived in Buckhead, Atlanta, in a hotel, had culture nights and watched each other's movies and ate each other's food from India, Korea, Jamaica, and other parts of the world. I had been exposed to a lot of difference throughout my life, and now I was going to do something to help others be exposed as well.

My speaking and workshops have been one way I have done that, and now this book will become another (albeit almost twenty years later). These were all stops along my journey to developing an Inclusive Mindset.

MY APPROACH TO THIS BOOK

I do not write this as one who has all the answers or has figured it all out. I am still struggling to understand it all, and I hope that what I have learned from my *many* failures can help you. There are many more people who know way more, are more compassionate, and are more inclusive than I am, and I salute them for teaching me on my own cultivation journey. I do want to apologize up front if I use the wrong term, say something that is not inclusive, or offend some. It is not my intention, and I always want to hear from you on this so I can grow and develop. This book won't be perfect, because I am not, but I will do my best to be as inclusive as possible while journeying through it with you. You may not always agree with me (and that's okay), but I hope you will challenge yourself to hear my heart as I share my research and passion with you.

I recognize that my approach will work for some but will not necessarily work for all. Some will read this book and say I didn't go far (or hard) enough, and some will say I went too far (or hard). There is no one-size-fits-all approach to true diversity and inclusion, and I feel we need them all (well, most of them). There are many approaches to cultivate diversity in our lives, and while I was arrogant early in my diversity and inclusion journey, now I am more open to differing approaches; mine is just one approach.

I am not going to spend a lot of time on the newest research (even though I will provide some) or on all of the terms like *equity*, *belonging*, and *social justice*, to name a few. While these terms are important (see "Additional Resources" at the end of the book for a link to a current list of these terms), my focus is on what I call the heart of the issue. I want people to grow in their knowledge but also to be inspired in their hearts. Even in my presentations I normally don't focus on all of the numbers or exact terminology (unless the client requests it), but rather on the heart of the message and helping people to not only get it but also internalize it. I don't want people to feel like diversity and inclusion are big initiatives; I want them to see them as a way of everyday living. I want them to see them not as a mandate but as a mindset.

HOW TO GET THE MOST OUT OF THIS BOOK

"Homogeneity isn't better; it's just easier."[4] I ask you to lean into this book, and while I do believe this book will be inspiring, it will also cause you to deeply reflect and feel uncomfortable. One of my favorite historical heroes is Frederick Douglass, who famously shared that "without struggle there is no progress."[5] I want this book to bring about big progress not only in your life but also in your workplace, in your community, and in our society. There are sections of the book that are uncomfortable for me to write as I approach it vulnerably, and there are things I share and struggle with that I am not proud of. But I believe we cannot truly grow unless we are real. I sometimes like to say that *pretending isn't progress*! I don't want to pretend with you, and I ask that you don't pretend as you take this journey with me.

Each chapter contains something for the head, heart, and hand. The head is some knowledge or piece of research. The heart is stories and anecdotes to cause you to feel what I am saying and not just understand what I am saying. The hand focuses on things you can actually do to progress forward. I ask you to be vulnerable as I will be vulnerable. I ask you to focus on progress, not perfection. You and I both have many areas where we need to grow, but what I have found is that when we focus on perfection it sometimes limits us from fully engaging. Last but not least, I ask you to take meaningful action. It won't always be mistake-free. It won't always feel good, but we owe it to ourselves and those around us to make an effort.

The stories I share in the book are real-life stories. I find it helpful to better understand the journey of others, and over the last decade I have heard some pretty amazing stories. I called some of those people and asked them to share about the successes and failures they've experienced along their Inclusive Mindset journeys, and I've included their stories here (some names have been changed to preserve the interviewees' privacy). I hope, like me, that you are inspired and challenged by these stories to progress in developing an Inclusive Mindset.

This book is not centered on organizational diversity and inclusion efforts (there are a lot of great books on this topic), but rather on how you as an individual can grow and progress in areas of diversity and inclusion to value people, expand your circles, and engage with those who are different in whatever ways they are different. I've included a guide to growing as intentionally inclusive leaders in the appendix, as I do recognize its importance, but it is not the focus of this book (maybe the next one). At the end I have also included how I work with organizations to move the needle in areas of diversity and inclusion (theinclusivemindsetorg.com). This book is also not exhaustive, as I could write entire books on almost every chapter, and there are volumes of other amazing books that expand on the topics we will discuss. Please check out the link in the "Additional Resources" section at the back of the book to dive deeper into each of the topics.

HOW TO START

Start right where you are. You have the ability to go somewhere very exciting with really interesting people. One of the challenges I have seen in our society is that we misconstrue strength-based ideology. To be clear, I believe in focusing on your strengths, but sometimes people confuse things they are not *yet* good at with a weakness. Think about a time when you couldn't do something well or you couldn't get a concept at work, but over time and with practice and effort you got better, improved, or perhaps did something you never thought you could do. Now all you have to do is think about diversity and inclusion like that.

In matters of diversity and inclusion, do you think you can grow, get better, and become more knowledgeable? How you answer this question will have a profound impact on how you approach this book. For some of you this may be an easy yes, but I also know that many of you are unsure, and I want to reassure you that you can definitely grow . . . because I have and many of my clients have. It won't be easy. It won't be without reflection, but it will be meaningful, and your outlook will improve more and more as you continue to put forth effort.

I have high standards for you. I believe you will be better after this book than when you started. Meaningful progress will begin or continue, as this is a journey, not an end. Let me affirm you: Diversity and inclusion are for you. Yes, even you. You can grow to have an Inclusive Mindset, as it is not reserved for special people with fancy degrees, or people in certain areas of the country or the world, or people who grew up with "diversity," but it is for you right now, where you are. So what are you waiting for? Let's grow!

ACTION FORWARD

1. Write down your honest thoughts when you hear the terms *diversity* and *inclusion* and how your past experiences have shaped that perspective.

2. Write down one area you want to grow in as it relates to diversity and inclusion.

3. What is one way your life has been positively impacted by diversity and inclusion (either something happening for you or something you did for someone else)?

Chapter 2

THE SECRET REVEALED

The One Thing That Must Happen to Cultivate Diversity Every Day

In 2019, I embarked on a journey like no other. A journey that would take my mental, emotional, spiritual, and physical dedication. A journey to get fit and healthier. Yes, I had taken this journey several times before, and it lasted for a short while, but this time I wanted to do something different. I wasn't going to start a crazy diet plan. I wasn't going to go to the gym on January 2, not to return for 365 days. I challenged myself to do something every day no matter what and no matter where I was. This challenge was a hundred-push-up challenge every day for three months. I read the literature on habit formation, and it showed that to start forming a habit it took not thirty days or even sixty days but rather between sixty-six and eighty-eight days. I really wanted exercise to be something I just did, not something I had to think about doing.

I've done almost everything from spin classes to CrossFit (yep, I'm one of those) to P90X. I would lose weight, get healthier, eat healthier, and then revert back to my old ways and gain the weight right back. I was living my own version of *The Biggest Loser*. The hundred-push-up challenge "pushed" me to see working out and eating somewhat healthy as a way of life and not something extra that I had to do at some point during the week. I believe that in those ninety days I only missed two days. I even did push-ups when I was in an airport waiting to board a plane to Ghana. People were wondering what was wrong with me, but I didn't care. I was determined to be different.

As of today I have lost over thirty pounds and some body fat, but more importantly, I feel healthier than I ever have. Exercise and eating healthy are just what I do now. I still eat the occasional food that isn't going to best fuel me, and while I am eating it, I am thinking about how the food will impact my day and my workouts. Also, when I don't work out, I feel like something is missing. While my weight still fluctuates, I am slowly progressing and have not returned to my starting weight and body fat. It is because these habits have become a part of my everyday life. They're who I am now.

Do you have a similar story? One that might not be fitness related but could be reading, cooking, gratitude, meditating, or journaling? What was the difference this time from the others? Let me let you in on a little secret . . .

WHAT'S THE SECRET?

What if I shared with you that there is only *one* thing you need to do in order to live an everyday life of diversity and inclusion? Would you believe me? I think many people overthink it and in the process psych themselves out of making meaningful progress. In my conversations, coaching, and presentations, I have noticed a common factor among those who "got it" and those who did not. No, it wasn't if they went to college, or grew up in certain parts of the country, or went to the once-in-a-lifetime training that would finally unlock the mysterious hidden world of diversity and inclusion.

The biggest difference for sustained change was in their approach. It wasn't some big initiative, but something they chose to do and be every day. They saw making the change not as a mandate but rather as a mindset. Something that would shape how they lived and experienced the world. That's the secret. How you approach engaging diversity and inclusion is vital to how you live it and cultivate it in your everyday life. The good news is that everything I share with you is something you are able to develop. There is significant research that supports the idea that we can grow in these areas if we choose to. I am elated that both you and I are not stuck with what we currently know and do, but that we can cultivate these areas in our lives. We can grow, get better, and develop new skills, and that is exciting, my friend.

CULTIVATION AT WORK

Do you believe that everyone, regardless of their beliefs, backgrounds, and behaviors, has inherent worth—that each person as a human being is valuable? You're reading this book, so you probably answered yes to that question, at least on a hypothetical level. But think about this: How does your view of a person change when you discover you disagree with them on a major issue or foundational belief? Does it become more difficult to see them as valuable? Have you ever felt devalued because you were different from someone else? The Inclusive Mindset starts from the approach that each person is valuable despite their differences. But saying we believe that is one thing; challenging ourselves to continue learning about and understanding the people we disagree with is a much bigger task that requires cultivation. This is the work of integrating diversity and inclusion into our lives.

Some of the definitions of *cultivate* in Dictionary.com are (1) "to promote or improve the growth of (a plant, crop, etc.) by labor and attention," (2) "to develop or improve by education or training," and (3) "to promote the growth or development of (an art, science, etc.); foster."[1] Often we see the word *cultivate* in reference to plants or crops, requiring work, spending time with, consistently tending to. The same thing must happen as we move to have diversity and inclusion as a part of our everyday lives. These qualities aren't going to mysteriously appear overnight. It isn't going to all make sense because we go to one training session (or read this one book), but as we practice the Inclusive Mindset, over time it will become a natural part of what we do. Digging, planting, pruning, cutting, watering are all things that become a consistent pattern of our lives.

What's the difference between a real plant and a fake one? One takes effort and cultivation and is living, while the other one may look good but is not living and takes no work. I have noticed that many people (including me) spend so much trying to prove that they are good people with really good intentions that they stay away from anything that would compromise that view, and thus they play it safe. We try to look good on the outside without doing the work of being truly healthy on the inside. Fake plants don't require intentionality, but they also can't produce vegetables or fruits. Fake plants may look good, but they don't have the same health benefits as the real thing. Putting in the work to truly change the way you see and interact with others who are different from you will be worth it.

WHY MINDSET MATTERS

What is a mindset anyway? This word has been used in so many different ways that maybe its meaning has been lost on us. J. D. Meier, director of innovation at Microsoft, says,

Your mindset is your collection of thoughts and beliefs that shape your thought habits. And your thought habits affect how you think, what you feel, and what you do. Your mindset impacts how you make sense of the world, and how you make sense of you.

Your mindset is a big deal.

Because they are related to mindset, it also helps to understand attitude and beliefs.[2]

To try to make it even simpler, it is how you see and experience the world; it is how you approach everyday life.

Having the right mindset won't mean things are always easy, but it will give you an inclination toward a direction. That's why in my coaching, conversations, and workshops with people I focus on ways to make diversity and inclusion a part of our everyday lives. My focus isn't making people the most intellectually astute on all the newest terms, ideas, and acronyms, but rather encouraging and challenging people to make those things a way of life. I want you to see *diversity and inclusion not as something that you have to do, but rather as something you choose to live.* What's powerful about mindset is that you can shift it. You aren't born with it; it's something that needs to be cultivated.

THE SOCIETAL MINDSET

Have you ever played with a Rubik's Cube? For those who don't know, a Rubik's Cube is a 3D puzzle made up of small squares of six different colors. The goal is to get all the colors to match on each of the six sides. I have never figured out how to do that thing . . . partly because I haven't really tried. If you're like me, you probably haven't figured out how to solve it either. But a person's ability to solve it somehow indicates their IQ in our society. And not just solving it but also how quickly you can solve it. There is even a whole documentary focused on Rubik's Cube international competitions and how quickly the cube can be solved. As of this writing the world record for the fastest solving of a Rubik's Cube is 4.22 seconds. (It took me longer to type "4.22 seconds" than it took the world record holder to solve the cube.)

You are celebrated if you can solve the Rubik's Cube really fast, as well as if you can do it blindfolded, behind your back, underwater, while bungee jumping, with your feet, with your left pinky toe underwater while suspended upside down feet away from a shark (well, maybe not this one . . . but someone may actually try this soon). When is the last time you saw someone praised or on the news because it took them five years to solve the Rubik's Cube? That is not what our society prioritizes. It prioritizes how fast you can do something compared to other people instead of praising the effort it takes to actually accomplish something. What would society look like if we could embrace progress over perfection?

GROWTH VERSUS A FIXED MINDSET

In describing the difference between a growth mindset and a fixed mindset, Stanford University psychologist Carol Dweck wrote, "In one world, effort is a bad thing. It, like failure, means you're not smart or talented. If you were, you wouldn't need effort. In the other world, effort is what *makes* you smart or talented."[3] Unfortunately, our society has created a culture where people are afraid to fail as it relates to diversity and inclusion, so some simply do not try at all in an effort to protect their image or perceived intelligence. We can no longer afford to do this, because real growth and progress don't happen when we are in protection mode.

A Growth Mindset

According to Dweck, a growth mindset is not about immediate perfection but rather about learning over time. It sees each experience as an opportunity to get better. It confronts challenge and is more focused on meaningful effort and progress than being the best and achieving perfection. Someone with a growth mindset isn't focused on doing things fast for the short-term but getting better for the long-term. In her book *Mindset,* Dweck writes, "People with the growth mindset know that it takes time for potential to flower."[4] Here are a few of the best descriptions that Dweck gives for a growth mindset:

- "Those with the growth mindset found success in doing their best, in learning and improving."[5]
- "People in a growth mindset don't just seek challenge, they thrive on it!"[6]
- "The growth mindset is the belief that abilities can be cultivated."[7]
- "Clearly, people with the growth mindset thrive when they're stretching themselves."[8]

The reason a growth mindset is so vital to the Inclusive Mindset is because cultivating diversity in our everyday lives is a choice to take a risk. Why do you think more people don't make this choice? I believe they don't make it for both internal and external reasons. Internally people shy away from the discomfort risk brings, and externally they don't feel it's safe to fail, or they might be unaware of areas where they need growth or help. Dweck shares,

Why waste time proving over and over how great you are, when you could be getting better? Why hide deficiencies instead of overcoming them? Why look for friends or partners who will just shore up your self-esteem instead of ones who will also challenge you to grow? And why seek out the tried and true, instead of experiences that will stretch you?[9]

I try my best to live this quote out in my everyday life. One of the things I always say is "Why settle for being the best when you can be better?" How we grow and progress is paramount to how we grow in matters of diversity and inclusion. Instead of defending who we perceive ourselves to be, we might consider focusing on how we get better little by little.

A Fixed Mindset

According to Dweck, a fixed mindset is all about the outcome. "If you fail—or if you're not the best—it's all been wasted. The growth mindset allows people to value what they're doing *regardless of the outcome*."[10] People in the fixed mindset think effort is reserved for those who don't have ability, and if you have to work at it, then you must not be good at it. Here are a few ways Dweck describes the fixed mindset:

- "Effort is only for people with deficiencies."[11]
- "The idea of trying and still failing—of leaving yourself without excuses—is the worst fear within the fixed mindset."[12]
- "The fixed mindset does not allow people the luxury of becoming. They have to already be."[13]
- "When you're given a positive label, you're afraid of losing it, and when you're hit with a negative label, you're afraid of deserving it."[14]

The reason the fixed mindset is so harmful to the Inclusive Mindset is because people in the fixed mindset operate within safety and focus on things they feel proficient at, which leads to less curiosity and trying new experiences because it is not safe. If something poses a challenge for people with a fixed mindset, they might feel it is calling into question their intelligence, and therefore they avoid it or do not fully engage. People do not like to perceive themselves as stupid or lacking intelligence.

Imagine a Fortune 500 CEO or a president of a university who has climbed the ranks of corporate America, sits on powerful boards, influences the world of trading, and yet feels insufficient to handle matters of diversity and inclusion. If he is operating from a fixed mindset, he is unlikely to take meaningful action (unless forced by societal and economic pressures) to transform the company's culture. He may be afraid to fail and reveal his lack of knowledge in this area, so it may be easier to relegate this to an HR function or put all of the responsibility on a newly appointed head of diversity and inclusion (or belonging, equity, or some newer term). I believe this is one of the reasons we have not been able to move the needle of diversity and inclusion in organizations.

Leading through the Two Mindsets

In talking about promoting a growth versus fixed mindset in others, Carol Dweck states, "I will judge and punish you? Or I will help you think and learn."[15] The person who is doing the judging and punishing is the one who has a fixed mindset and either assumes someone else can't learn or doesn't create the safety necessary for that person to learn. The person who believes that others can change, think, and learn—and creates space for that change in themselves and others—has a growth mindset. Not only does your mindset determine what you personally believe and how you act, but it also impacts how you interact with others and how they may respond.

I used to operate primarily in the fixed mindset. A few years ago, I visited a potential preschool for my daughter, and while I was on the tour I asked one of the teachers about their efforts to create a more diverse and inclusive environment. The teacher's response: "Oh, that's not a big deal for me because I am color-blind." And she didn't mean she couldn't tell red from green. I was baffled. I was dumbfounded. I wondered how she could even think this way. I wondered what was wrong with her. I didn't want her to be color-blind but rather to see my color (my race) as something positive and devoid of the usual negative stereotypes. Unfortunately, what I did not do was try to understand her perspective.

I failed to recognize in the moment that the teacher was trying to communicate her acceptance of all people, albeit by using an outdated term. "Being color-blind" used to be seen as a good thing.

It was used as a way to communicate that people were more accepting and open to people of all races. This teacher hadn't learned that *color-blind* isn't widely used today and isn't seen as a positive thing, and unfortunately in my judgment I did not take the time to share that with her. I believed she would never understand or that she should know that already. But when I looked in the mirror and thought about the issues of my Mexican brothers and sisters, or issues of the First Peoples (Native Americans), or issues of those with various disabilities of which I was ignorant, I recognized that I was probably using outdated terminology and that I would want grace. Instead, I was extending judgment to this woman at the preschool. I could have shared with her (in private) another term or way to approach how she saw people of different races, but I myself was operating in a fixed mindset.

While growth mindset people "learn from and repair their failure, people with the fixed mindset may simply try to repair their self-esteem. For example, they may go looking for people who are even worse off than they are."[16] This is where you get people who say, "At least I'm not as bad as they are, or at least I don't do _____." This gives us at times an excuse not to progress and grow in diversity and inclusion within our own lives. It is much easier to deflect and criticize than to reflect and grow. Again, often because we want to protect our image with others.

This sentiment was reinforced in a study conducted by Carol Dweck in which she interviewed students from the University of Hong Kong, where everything is in English, and found that "students with the fixed mindset were so worried about appearing deficient that they refused to take a course that would improve their English." When Dweck and her researchers gave the students hard problems to solve and then asked them to write a letter to someone in another school sharing their experience in the study, they noticed that almost 40 percent of the students lied about their scores being higher than they were. They wanted to have an image that was better than their scores illustrated.[17]

Many of us do this in our everyday lives. When we enter new friendships or relationships, we show people our "representative" selves instead of the person who is flawed, insecure, and sometimes feels like an imposter. In order to grow and develop in matters of diversity and inclusion, we must approach ourselves and others authentically. As you learn about real diversity, remember that having a growth mindset is important for both yourself and the people you engage.

ACTION FORWARD

1. Take the Birthday Challenge. Identify one thing you have never done but always thought about doing and accomplish it by your next birthday. (Examples: Learning to ski, learning a new language, learning to cook twelve dishes, running a marathon, taking a photography class)

2. Start each day acknowledging the progress and effort you undertook.

3. Identify one thing you initially were not good at but over time became much better at. What happened and how did you get better?

Chapter 3

DIVERSITY REDEFINED

Diving into Difference

When you first see or hear the word *diversity*, what do you think of? Do you think of race, sexuality, gender, religion, politics, disabilities, trainings, affirmative action, age, country of origin? I sometimes ask this question when I work with organizations, and when people are being honest and trying not to be politically correct, they share these as a first thought. I'm not asking what the real definition is, but what you think of when you see or hear the word *diversity*. While these areas are part of diversity, they are not diversity in its simplest form.

Diversity in its simplest form is just difference. Can you come from the same place, look very similar, and still be very different? An emphatic *yes!* What I have realized after more than a decade of work in this field is that while many of these micro-areas are important (and some more important at times within specific nations), many people have not learned how to value difference for difference's sake (the macro). I hypothesized that if that value is not in place, it will be much harder to encourage people to embrace the micro-differences as something not to ostracize or run from but rather to cultivate in their everyday lives. I've come to understand that there are a lot of people who have great head knowledge about diversity and inclusion, but very few who have heart knowledge, and I believe the heart level is where true and long-lasting transformation occurs.

DIVERSITY IS . . .

Merriam-Webster defines *diversity* as "the condition of having or being composed of differing elements: VARIETY; *especially* the inclusion of people of different races . . . [or] cultures . . . in a group or organization."[1] This is the macro-definition of diversity, and I believe it is helpful and healthy for people to build a foundation on the macro as they work to grow and learn in the micro-areas.

Do you see yourself as part of this important work, or have you felt like issues of diversity and inclusion just aren't your thing? Have you even thought that diversity and inclusion don't apply to you? Unfortunately, in some of my presentations there are some who have come up to me afterward and shared that this was the first time they felt included in a diversity and inclusion conversation. This has and continues to break my heart. Everyone is invited to the table (now, some have to learn to listen more than they share, but we should all be at the table together working toward a common good). This is not something for "those" people to figure out and do. This is something for all of us to work toward because we all have unique things about us that make us different.

Diversity is also all the words that are associated with it. To me it is the umbrella of things like inclusion, belonging, equity and equality, and being an ally. Real diversity was never meant to be representation, quotas, or variety in our workplaces and on our boards just for the sake of looking diverse. Diversity was never meant to be representation without inclusion, counting without consideration, and increasing numbers without increasing a sense of belonging. When diversity began to be misused and misunderstood, many of the other terms were created to highlight the nuances within the diversity conversation. This is why you now see *diversity* and *inclusion* paired together so often, and why I've paired them together in this book and my presentations.

DIVERSITY IS NOT . . .

Diversity is not sitting at the campfire singing "Kumbaya" or holding hands singing Queen Latifah's rendition of "U.N.I.T.Y" or "We Are the World." I see many people put an emphasis on diversity as agreeing with everyone. The goal of real diversity is not that we will always agree, but rather that when we disagree I can still respect you. It is when I can vehemently disagree with your ideology but passionately pursue your humanity. That, my friend, is real diversity. One thing I have learned is that everyone loves diversity . . . as long as it is their brand of diversity. As long as we agree about all the same things, then people embrace diversity. There are always going to be things we disagree on, and that is okay, but one thing we cannot and should not disagree on is valuing the humanity of every individual.

Diversity is not just the "big three": gender, race, and sexuality. Sometimes when people say we need diversity, this is what they are referring to. When I watched the primary elections in 2020, I heard political pundits talking about how when we get past Iowa and New Hampshire, we will get to the "diverse" states. *What does that mean?* There is plenty of diversity in Iowa and New Hampshire (yes, I have been to both). Now, what I believe they meant was that there may not be as much racial diversity or ethnic diversity in those states as other states, but there is certainly diversity at a macrolevel. That's why when we're talking about diversity and being diverse, it is important to use what I call the *prefix*. This is the word you place before *diversity* to describe what type of diversity you are specifically mentioning. Beyond the big three you can have ability diversity, religious diversity, cultural diversity, age diversity, and the list goes on. When we define diversity as only the big three, it can send the message to some that they are not a part of the diversity conversation, when the truth is that all of us are a part of this conversation.

Diversity is not one person. As a former recruiter I remember constantly hearing that we need more diverse talent. *What does that mean?* One of my informal mentors in the diversity space is Susan Johnson, chief diversity officer at the Hartford, who once shared, "One of my pet peeves is when people talk about diverse talent. A person cannot be diverse by themselves." The very definition of diversity is variety and requires at least two things that are different. You may desire more gender diversity, racial diversity, religious diversity, or ability diversity, but diversity is not and cannot be a person by themselves.

Diversity is also not just about you or me. As I have traveled across the world, I have found that most people do not believe in diversity at all. They believe in what I call "diversi-me." That simply means the *only* thing that has value is my specific difference. I am not saying that your and my specific differences don't have value, but if that is the only thing we ever focus on and give energy to, that is not valuing real diversity.

Even if you are part of a marginalized or underrepresented group, there are other marginalized and underrepresented groups. This does not mean you have to focus on every aspect of diversity, or ignore issues that relate to you, but one thing I encourage people to do is find one thing they can advocate for that has relatively nothing to do with them. An example of that is a focus I am growing into around gender equity in the workplace. I am not a woman, and as a male I have experienced certain privileges that many of my female colleagues may not have experienced (for example, the pay gap). There is so much I do not know, but I continue despite my ignorance. Realizing that I am ignorant in certain areas helps me better understand the challenges to learning something new and stepping up for others when it doesn't directly affect me. Being able and willing to stand up for others is one reason why diversity and inclusion are vital.

WHY DIVERSITY AND INCLUSION ARE IMPORTANT

I have been hearing more and more that diversity doesn't matter. That it is a leftist agenda, that it is simply brainwashing, or that it is ruining the world. I believe those sentiments to be false, partly because my definition of diversity involves all of us and takes all of us to move it forward. Diversity and inclusion are super important because at their core they're about treating others with respect and value.

The Business Case

A *business case* is something that "captures the reasoning for initiating a project or task. It is often presented in a well-structured written document but may also come in the form of a short verbal agreement or presentation. The logic of the business case is that, whenever resources such as money or effort are consumed, they should be in support of a specific business need."[2]

The established business case is one reason to prioritize diversity and inclusion in not only your personal life but also your professional life. Extensive studies and research have shown how diversity and inclusion are important for organizations. Here's what McKinsey & Company, a leading voice of research in this area, has found:

> While not causal, we observe a real relationship between diversity and performance that has persisted over time and across geographies. There are clear and compelling

hypotheses for why this relationship persists, including improved access to talent, enhanced decision making and depth of consumer insight, and strengthened employee engagement and license to operate.[3]

In other words, good things happen in diverse organizations. And while not every positive outcome could be attributed to diversity, the case could be made for diversity supporting a business in prospering. In 2020 McKinsey & Company reported the following:

> Over the past five years, the likelihood that diverse companies will out-earn their industry peers has grown. So have the penalties for companies lacking diversity. . . .
>
> For example, several reports have shown that in the 2008–09 global financial crisis, banks with a higher share of women on their boards were more stable than their peers. . . .
>
> Our research has demonstrated that organizations investing in diversity and inclusion are strongly positioned in this regard, in part because diversity brings multiple perspectives to bear on problems, thereby boosting the odds of more creative solutions. Diverse companies are also more likely to have employees who feel they can be themselves at work and are empowered to participate and contribute.[4]

McKinsey reported that companies spend $8 billion on diversity training, but many experts say there is little evidence it has moved the needle.[5] Moving the needle goes beyond head knowledge and how it can make the organization more profitable. While the business case is important and helpful, it isn't the only reason professionals should prioritize diversity and inclusion. Actually, it shouldn't even be the place where we start. In the appendix ("How to Be an Intentionally Inclusive Leader"), I argue for a more in-depth focus on what I call the humanity case. When the business case is the primary driver, people are seen as commodities, and people who are underrepresented or marginalized don't want to be included just because it can help organizations make better decisions, have more of a competitive advantage, and ultimately increase profitability, but rather because individuals are qualified and because it is the right and decent thing to do.

Including people because it's the right thing to do should be the driving force. But why should it be important for you as an individual? Those who begin to cultivate diversity and inclusion in their everyday lives experience a richness in relationships, an openness to ideas that are different, and a different type of learning. Again, not always agreement, but an appreciation for the other human beings involved. At the end of the day I believe you want to be treated with decency and considered valuable, and that is pretty much what others want too.

Beyond the Business Case

I am often asked by CEOs and executives how they can better "diversify" their organizations. While I am grateful for and appreciative of the desire to do this, my first response has nothing to do with their organization at all, but rather with their personal lives. I ask them, "Who are your friends? Who do you have lunches and dinners with, or have over to your house? Who do you learn from, who are your mentors, and who can influence your life in meaningful ways?" If those people all fit the same demographic, then it is unlikely that deep and meaningful progress will be made within the organization over the long haul.

Our relationships matter, because how our hearts are impacted, not just our heads, shapes how we move forward. What about you? I ask you the same question I ask CEOs, executives, and leaders. Who is in your life, and do your relationships reflect the kind of specific diversity you would like and/or want (we will get into this more in chapter 5)? Diversity and inclusion are not just about what you do at work but about what you do at home and in your community!

Focusing on the heart level and how diversity and inclusion impact your personal life isn't abnormal, because for many people the personal aspect is the primary driver to pursue diversity and inclusion. A recent article by Deloitte, a leading audit and consulting firm, says, "Intriguingly, however, many of the leaders interviewed in our research cited the extrinsic reward of enhanced performance as a secondary motivator. Their primary motivation for pursuing diversity and inclusion was alignment with their own personal values and a deep-seated sense of fairness."[6] The article continues, "This insight is consistent with research by the US-based think tank Catalyst, which identified 'a strong sense of fair play' as the most significant predictor that men would champion gender initiatives in the workplace. Interestingly, Catalyst also observed that individuals' 'commitment to fairness ideals was rooted in very personal experiences.'"[7] These personal experiences shape the professional experiences people have, so maybe more focus should be given to helping facilitate the personal experiences so that the professional experiences become more than lip service and a tidy well-put-together statement.

This is consistent with how change management expert John Kotter sees long-lasting change occurring.

> This combination of intellect (that is, belief in the business case) and emotion (that is, a sense of fair play and caring for people as individuals, not "resources") is consistent with the "head and heart" strategy emphasized by change expert John Kotter. According to Kotter, while engaging the minds of individuals through rational arguments is important, "people change what they do less because they are given analysis that shifts their thinking than because they are shown a truth that influences their feelings."[8]

So why are diversity and inclusion important? Because they concern people like you and me. They impact all of us directly and indirectly, and every person has value, dignity, and worth (yes, even those we disagree with). When we cultivate an Inclusive Mindset in our hearts and our daily lives, we can engage with the world in a respectful and productive way as an outpouring of what we value.

ACTION FORWARD

1. How have you defined diversity in the past, and how does the foundational definition of diversity simply being difference impact how you look at it now?

2. Identify a community you're not directly involved with and begin learning about its past and present, and what you can do to support that group (for example, the deaf).

3. Ask three to five family members or friends how they define *diversity* and share your definition with them.

Chapter 4

DEFINING THE INCLUSIVE MINDSET

A Shift toward Everyday Life

There I was, skiing down the slopes (well, maybe the small ski hill) in Vail, Colorado, with some of my fraternity brothers. This was the culmination of my first birthday challenge, where I challenged myself to do one thing I had never done before but always thought about doing. As I stumbled onto the magic carpet (the escalator-type contraption for beginners), I was slightly embarrassed to see little kids who were five and six years old skiing like pros while I was falling, stumbling, and getting rather cold.

What possessed me to want to go skiing for the first time in my thirties? Why did I subject myself to such humiliation? Why was I on this magic carpet, which I perceived as a sign of beginners that would showcase my inability to ski? I did it because I wanted to grow, develop, and learn something new. *My fear of feeling stupid had to be overtaken by my excitement to learn something new.*

WHAT IS THE INCLUSIVE MINDSET?

While we have briefly talked about the Inclusive Mindset in the previous chapters, it is time for a deeper understanding of what it really is. The Inclusive Mindset is a willingness to approach each day with curiosity, openness, and a desire to treat people you meet with respect and dignity. It is an admission that perfection will never occur, and that progression is the focus. It is more concerned with growing in diversity and inclusion than it is with looking to others like you have it all together. It is diversity and inclusion mixed with a little growth mindset and meaningful action. It isn't merely about behavioral change (even though this is important), but it is rather a change in how you look at the world and the beautiful people in it. The Inclusive Mindset is a deeper understanding of others and their stories, history, challenges, and success.

The first step toward an Inclusive Mindset is accepting where you are currently with your thoughts, behaviors, and ideology—faults and all. After all, pretending doesn't help progress. The focus in the Inclusive Mindset is not necessarily where you have been but rather where you are currently, and even more important, where you are going. Where you are now does not represent where you can be, if you so choose. The Inclusive Mindset is something you have to work toward. Over time it becomes simply who you are.

Developing an Inclusive Mindset is learnable and is not pass or fail. It is something all of us can develop if we take the time to intentionally grow in it. In the Inclusive Mindset, each day you get better as you engage both the day and people with curiosity and wonder. You can grow in the Inclusive Mindset by trying new things, giving great effort, and utilizing others as a sounding board to assess how you are realistically doing. Real growth and learning requires research, asking questions, and admitting that you don't know and can use assistance.

I haven't met anyone who lives by the Inclusive Mindset 100 percent of the time. We all have times when we don't fully embrace the Inclusive Mindset (I know I have a *whole* lot of them). Some of us have those moments that are happening internally even if nothing is noticeable externally. It isn't something we live in 100 percent of the time, but rather something that challenges us to continue growing, even when we temporarily operate by the Exclusion Mindset.

WHAT IS THE EXCLUSION MINDSET?

The Exclusion Mindset is the opposite of the Inclusive Mindset and is more focused on proving that you are knowledgeable and understanding in areas of diversity and inclusion than growing in these areas. With the Exclusion Mindset you tend to spend more time proving what you know than actually learning about other people and perspectives. The Exclusion Mindset is focused on showing others how smart you are in diversity and inclusion or, on the other extreme, casting matters of diversity and inclusion as not important or something that does not require your focus or effort, rendering it essentially meaningless.

When you have the Exclusion Mindset you think the world needs to adapt to you, and you don't take ownership of your own inadequacies with issues relating to diversity and inclusion. The focus is on a whole bunch of things you know rather than having an eagerness to learn and keep growing.

An Inclusive Mindset is different from an Exclusion Mindset in ten key ways:

1. A person with the Inclusive Mindset focuses on trying new things even when difficult, while someone with the

Exclusion Mindset focuses on only engaging in conversations and experiences that are easy.

2. A person with the Inclusive Mindset takes initiative and an active role in diversity and inclusion growth, while someone with the Exclusion Mindset takes a passive approach and allows other people and organizations to drive the process.

3. A person with the Inclusive Mindset listens deeply to others in order to understand, while someone with the Exclusion Mindset listens to disagree and bolster their own argument.

4. A person with the Inclusive Mindset reflects, recognizes their faults, and seeks feedback from others, while someone with the Exclusion Mindset blames others and does not seek input from others.

5. A person with the Inclusive Mindset intentionally engages others who look, think, and believe differently, while someone with the Exclusion Mindset either leaves all their interactions to chance and/or only engages with those who look, think, and believe similarly.

6. A person with the Inclusive Mindset focuses on ways they can progress in their strengths and weaknesses in matters of diversity and inclusion, while someone with the Exclusion Mindset focuses on how to be perfect before they take action.

7. A person with the Inclusive Mindset doesn't compare themselves to others because they are focused on their own growth in diversity and inclusion (while still learning from others), while someone with the Exclusion Mindset generally compares themselves to those they perceive are worse than they are (i.e., "At least I am not as bad as . . .").

8. A person with the Inclusive Mindset risks their standing and others' perception of them when combatting

injustice or unfair treatment toward someone else, while someone with the Exclusion Mindset will stand up for others only if it is deemed safe and won't negatively impact them in others' eyes.

9. A person with the Inclusive Mindset looks for opportunities to invite others who are missing from the room (especially marginalized and underrepresented groups), while someone with the Exclusion Mindset focuses only on their own self-interests.

10. A person with the Inclusive Mindset acknowledges that good intent doesn't always translate to positive impact, while someone with the Exclusion Mindset thinks that just because they have good intentions, their missteps are not really a big deal.

THE INCLUSIVE MINDSET APPLIED IN SOCIETY

Why do you think people don't do meaningful things that will help them grow in diversity and inclusion? I believe it's often because in society people are judged as either competent or incompetent versus progressing. While it is true in some matters in our society people should be much further along than they are, it is also true that we can value and appreciate meaningful progress as it occurs. In the book *The Progress Principle*, authors Teresa Amabile and Steven Kramer share that people feel better and healthier about their work when they feel they are making meaningful progress, even if it's incremental.[1] Could this same principle apply to matters of diversity and inclusion? I believe if you focus on meaningful progress that you will feel better and healthier about your "work" in developing an Inclusive Mindset.

We've conditioned people to flee failure rather than face it. Many people choose to play it safe over making meaningful progress because they are afraid to fail. They are also afraid of hearing (1) "Why can't you get it right?" (2) "Come on, it's the twenty-first

century and you still don't know that?" (3) "You're sooooooooo
ignorant," or (4) "You are a _____ (racist, homophobe, ageist,
sexist, etc.)." We are quick to label people and give them little hope
for growth. Imagine if your child or a child you know couldn't
do a math problem. Would you berate them for getting it wrong
(maybe some parents would), or would you help them learn how
to do it? While people should take ownership of their own growth,
there also needs to be a group of people willing and able to help
others who don't get it. After all, change is hard.

In *Mindset*, Carol Dweck states, "Even when you change, the
old beliefs aren't just removed like a worn-out hip or knee and
replaced with better ones. Instead, the new beliefs take their place
alongside the old ones, and as they become stronger, they give you
a different way to think, feel, and act."[2] This isn't just in matters
of diversity and inclusion, but it is also in matters of our everyday
lives. Let me give you an example. Most of us know that good posture is sitting up straight, but many of us struggle to sit up straight
(I know you just straightened up—for now). It is important for
me to acknowledge the tension between real change needing to
happen for marginalized and underrepresented groups and the
opportunity for people to grow, make mistakes, and keep learning.
It is not one or the other; we must find a way for them to coexist in
order to help people develop an Inclusive Mindset.

The Inclusive Mindset is the ideal, and even those with an
Inclusive Mindset still discriminate, say or do the wrong things,
and make mistakes, but the difference is how they react to them
and move forward. *Again, the Inclusive Mindset isn't a call to be perfect but rather to have meaningful progress and growth in matters
of diversity and inclusion.* Here are a few questions you should ask
yourself to take steps closer to that progress: (1) Who can I learn
from or about that is different from me? (2) What can I do today to
make someone else feel included and valued? and (3) Where can
I step up for someone else who is either marginalized or underrepresented in my organization or community?

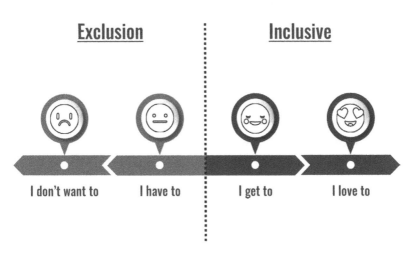

Inclusive/Exclusion Mindset Continuum™

Exclusion | **Inclusive**

I don't want to | I have to | I get to | I love to

We can all strive to be more like the "I love tos" on the Inclusive/Exclusion continuum. People who operate by the Exclusion Mindset approach diversity and inclusion with the perspective "I don't want to" because of reasons ranging from a fear of looking stupid to a lack of understanding of diversity and inclusion's true importance. People who operate by the Inclusive Mindset approach diversity and inclusion with an "I love to" perspective. Not that it will be easy or that they will agree with everything, but they see it as an opportunity to learn something new and highlight the inherit value others possess.

The remaining chapters will help you develop more of an Inclusive Mindset. They will offer practical tips and suggestions to inspire you to be more curious and learn more about others. You will learn how to better communicate, stand up for others, and enlarge your professional and personal circles. If you already have an Inclusive Mindset, you will be challenged to keep growing, and if you currently operate by an Exclusion Mindset, you will be inspired to grow and develop, starting right where you are.

ACTION FORWARD

1. Write down how you currently approach diversity and inclusion on the continuum.

2. Of the ten characteristics of an Inclusive Mindset, which are you currently doing well? Why is that the case?

3. With which characteristics of the Inclusive Mindset do you need the most help? What will you do to help improve those areas?

part two

DEVELOPING
AN INCLUSIVE
MINDSET

Chapter 5

CIRCLES OF GRACE™

Why We See People and Events the Way We Do and What to Do about It

I am a people watcher when I travel. Years ago I would watch people get on the plane and I would comment on their nice Michael Kors bag or their Yeezys (even though they may have been Cheezys and not real). One day I was sitting down on a plane, minding my own business (while watching people), and I saw this gentleman of what I thought was Middle Eastern descent wearing what some might deem "traditional" Islamic clothing. My posture didn't change, my facial expression didn't change, and not a word was uttered out of my mouth, but inside my mind I asked the question, *Am I safe?* Do you know who I didn't think that about? I didn't think that about the white businesswoman, the Latina, or the Black man. I then proceeded to have an internal conversation with myself, asking, *Justin, Inclusive Mindset guy, what's going on?* I realized I did not have anyone of his perceived identity in my Circles of Grace, and therefore I subconsciously accepted secondhand information I absorbed from the media.

WHAT ARE THE CIRCLES OF GRACE?

The Circles of Grace is a model I created nearly a decade ago when a major tragedy occurred in American society. When I turned to social media, it seemed like everyone had a different perspective on the event. I wondered how this one event could lead to such vastly different perspectives, and I began to dig into the research. I created this model based on research, specifically social isolation and its impact on sociocultural diversity (when we are isolated from people in other cultures, people groups, or ways of life, it impacts us). The Circles of Grace model is also influenced by similar-attraction theory, which states that the more a person perceives someone to be similar to them, the more they positively see this person.[1]

So who do we tend to give the most grace, the benefit of the doubt, more trust, and more leniency? You guessed right: you! We tend to give ourselves the most grace and benefit of the doubt (in general, as there are always exceptions to the rule). We know what we meant. We know if we were joking or being sarcastic. Generalization alert: we know if we were being Midwest nice (thanks, Nebraska), West Coast nice (it's cool), Southern nice (bless your heart), or Northeast nice (are you still in my face?).

Who comes after that in the next circle? Yep, right again: family and friends. That's why Lil Johnnie does something wrong, but Lil Johnnie's mom says, "Not my Lil Johnnie!" Lil Johnnie could have looked into the security camera and said, "Mom, I'm so sorry I did it," and Lil Johnnie's

mom would still say, "I don't know who that is. That must be Lil Johnnie's evil twin whom I did not know he had, because my Lil Johnnie would never have done this!" A person could have committed a heinous crime, and their friends and family would say, "I don't know how they could do this. They are just a good person!"

Who is next in the circle? People like you and people like those you love come next. That is why you hear someone say, "That could have been my son" or "That could have been my sister" or "That could have been my mom."

After that comes . . . everyone else. Where is everyone else? They are outside the Circles of Grace. They are given little to no grace, little to no benefit of the doubt; they are guilty until proven innocent. In the opening story I shared with you who my "everyone else" used to be. That story is nuanced, because I didn't have that same reaction when I saw Black people dressed in "traditional" Islamic clothing (I have several friends who are Black Muslims), or when I saw a person who appeared

to be from the Middle East wearing a "traditional" Western business suit, but only that specific combination of Middle Eastern descent and "traditional" Islamic clothing.

DON'T TAKE THE EXIT

When we do not have people in our Circles of Grace who fit a certain type of person or demographic, where do we tend to get information about them? We tend to get it from social media, the news, websites, and other second- and thirdhand conduits of information. Have you ever had people talk about you, but not to you? Don't you hate that? You might wonder why they didn't just say something to you. Oftentimes we do this to whole groups of people without malicious intent. We take second- and thirdhand information as absolute truth without talking to the people it's about. Unfortunately, our brains are wired that way.

There is research to suggest that our brains reserve energy for things it thinks it doesn't know or doesn't expect to experience. In an article by the University of Glasgow, the authors share about "a fairly new hypothesis developed by University College London neuroscientist Karl Friston called predictive coding—or free energy principle—which suggests the brain is actively predicting what input it will receive, rather than just passively processing information as it arrives."[2]

When you drive to work Monday through Friday, do you take the same exit? Day after day you take this exit, and sometimes you even take the exit on Saturdays too. Monday through Saturday you take this exit, and then one day you are supposed to go straight past the exit, but what do you do? You take the exit because your brain is on autopilot and predicting what you will do and experience next. It pulls up your normal pattern of going this certain way and thinks you will go that way again. That is similar to what we do with people. Right before we get to know who people really are, we take the exit of second- and thirdhand information that has been coded and categorized. We start to generalize or stereotype that these types of people are like this and value this, without ever really taking the time to find out if our assumptions are true. That is exactly what I did with the gentleman on the plane. I immediately took the exit to all the things I was seeing in movies, reading in the news, and hearing about men who looked like him.

I challenged myself to seek to be more interested than interesting. At the time I lived in a townhome community in Clinton, Mississippi, and several Saudi Arabian families lived there. I began striking up conversations and learning more about them and their journeys here. I learned that not everyone from Saudi Arabia is a Muslim, among many other revealing things. That experience and several others led me to believe that we can actually create one more circle: a circle of meaningful relationships and exposure.

DEVELOPING MEANINGFUL RELATIONSHIPS

The reason I say *meaningful* relationships is because it has to be deeper than "I have two white friends. Yay!" We have to be able to talk about the hard issues and come back to a place of trust. We often hear people say, "I have [a certain demographic] friends, and they have never shared that with me before." Sometimes some of our friends who are "different" have never experienced some of the typical challenges people in their demographic group have, and sometimes they have simply chosen not to share it with you in order to not be labeled or "othered."

I remember once doing a session with a good buddy of mine, Otis Pickett, for a youth group in Mississippi, and this youth group was predominantly white with one Black young man. We had some great conversations, and when we asked the Black young man if he had either felt racism or been discriminated against in life, he shared that in fact he had felt racism and been discriminated against, but he had never shared it with his youth group friends (even though he was close to them and saw them every week). He said he shared it with his other Black friends at school. A new phenomenon is happening with many of the racial injustices occurring in America where colleagues, classmates, and community members are now speaking up and sharing their experiences that they had previously reserved for people they thought would "get it."

It's also important to go beyond the sample size of one or two, because just because one person of that specific demographic has had that experience doesn't mean they speak for all people in that demographic. Not all people who have a disability share the same concerns, perspectives, and outlook. Not all Generation X people hate millennials. It is important to see those people as both individuals and part of a collective group. We are never done learning about people, and it is crucial that we approach people with a beginner's mind. In our relationships we should ask deeper questions and learn from each other's experiences, both good and bad.

One way to build meaningful relationships is to volunteer or join organizations where it is more likely that you will encounter people who are different. A warning: Don't start a relationship by asking every question about a person's demographic or differences, but value them simply as an individual. As you build trust and comradery, you may be able to branch out and ask deeper questions about their specific demographic. Trust is essential to having meaningful conversations. *It's not just about having diversity in your life; it's what you do with it that matters!*

James Robilotta and Iota Phi Theta

It was spring 2007, and James was finally crossing into the great fraternity of Iota Phi Theta, one of the nine fraternities and sororities that is historically Black (known as the Divine Nine). This wouldn't have been abnormal, except that James was not Black . . . he was white. While it is somewhat common to see a Black person join a predominantly white fraternity or sorority, it is less likely to see a white person join one of the Divine Nine organizations. When I talked with James in 2020, he shared that there were a number of people who thought only Black people should be in the Divine Nine, but James was inspired by the mission of the fraternity, touched by the friendships, and he connected to the values of Iota Phi Theta. Unknowingly he was enlarging his circles and would forever have a brotherhood with those who, while different in race, were similar in mission. James continues to cultivate relationships inside and outside the fraternity, and he is constantly engaging new people and new experiences. He says, "Individuals who are done learning are done living!"[3]

EXPOSURE AND THE SIX-MONTH CHALLENGE™

Not only are meaningful relationships helpful in constant learning (and living), but exposing others to new and different people is also helpful in enlarging our circles. Unfortunately, what I often find is that we tend to confine our lives to our circles of comfort. We only really engage people like us or those who make us feel safe and don't threaten our ideology or way of seeing the world. If you disagree with me, I delete you, unfriend you, and unfollow you. I do not believe we can have a rich experience of learning if everyone we interact with already agrees with us on matters that are important to us. I am not talking about potentially trivial matters like which NFL or college football team you like (even though I know people who will not marry a person who likes certain teams), but rather things that are deeply important to you.

One way to expose yourself beyond your circles of comfort is to take the Six-Month Challenge™. The Six-Month Challenge is something I challenge myself to do every six months, where I go to an event (live or virtual), experience something, or engage with someone I either disagree with or don't know a lot about. One of my most transformative Six-Month Challenges was going to a mosque to hear a Qur'anic scholar. I learned so much I didn't know, and I heard some really interesting things I agreed with, even things that challenged some of my previously held beliefs. I also heard things I still disagreed with. I did not walk out of the mosque a Muslim, but going there allowed me to see the humanity of people. It allowed me to get firsthand information and learn.

When you do a Six-Month Challenge, you should go asking two main questions: (1) What did I learn about this event, experience, or person? and (2) What did I learn about myself as I engaged that event, experience, or person? What about you? When have you really taken time to learn from someone or a group of people that you either disagreed with or did not know a lot about?

There are things you can do in your everyday life to help facilitate this, like reading or watching news from outlets you normally wouldn't pay attention to in order to get a more well-rounded perspective. Listen to radio programs that might offer a differing perspective than you hold. Join or participate in an ERG (employee resource group) that is made up of people who are different from you. Take stock of your current friends and their possible differences, such as mental health, ability, country of origin, faith, race, gender, and many of the other micro-areas of diversity, and have meaningful conversations where you are learning from their perspectives.

After George Floyd was killed, several friends reached out to me and asked about my experience as a Black man in America, and they took time to listen. When Ghana opened up dual-citizenship, several friends reached out to me and asked about my experience as a Ghanaian American and what it was like growing up. I've also taken the initiative to reach out to some of my friends who hold different political views than I do so I can learn from them. I've talked to friends who are police officers to hear their perspectives and views of what's going on in society. I have reached out to some of my gay friends and my female friends to hear their journeys and perspectives. Not all my conversations have been easy, and at times I've had to apologize for how I reacted, but overall, I am learning and continuing to take ownership and an active role in my growth and development in areas of diversity and inclusion. I am not perfect, but I am progressing. I have been vulnerable with you, so I am curious to know, who is your everyone else?

WHO IS YOUR "EVERYONE ELSE"?

Who are the people you tend to give no grace, no benefit of the doubt? Are they guilty until proven innocent? What do they watch on TV? What political parties do they belong to? Who did they vote for or who did they support? What do they look like? What part of the country are they from, if they are from this country at all? What marches do they go to? Where do they go on Sunday, or Saturday, or Friday if they choose to go anywhere at all? How do they identify?

This is one of the parts of my presentation where people start getting a little uncomfortable or, to the other extreme, self-righteous. If you are thinking to yourself, *Justin, I do not have an "everyone else." I just love everybody* (spirit fingers), well, I hate to burst your bubble, but every single one of us, including me, has an everyone else, if not several. Every single one of us has bias, both conscious and unconscious. Knowingly or unknowingly, we have ways that we look at people.

So again, I ask you, who is your "everyone else"?

Here's a hint: your everyone else is not a single person (stop pointing). That person may hold to an ideology that you disdain or disagree with, or may represent a certain group of people, but a single person is not your everyone else. Here are a few examples I have heard and experienced in my presentations. I once heard a Southern male share that Northerners were his everyone else because they sometimes thought he was dumb just because he spoke with a Southern accent. Another example was people who are only interested in networking with people they think can do something for them (actually, that might be another of my everyone elses). People shared that it felt very transactional and not relational when someone only wants to talk to you if they think you are valuable to something they are trying to do.

Sometimes people will only share about a bias they have gotten over. But we're talking about current bias here. Let me share one that I still struggle with. Whenever I see a Black woman who is in a romantic relationship with a white male, my automatic reaction is, "Oh, there are not enough good brothers for you." Now, I know that to be wrong, and people can choose who they want to love. Several friends of mine are Black women who are in romantic relationships with white males (including my current business manager), but that doesn't stop my conditioned response that was built up over a few decades. You see, in certain parts of my family, that was not accepted. In my neighborhood growing up, that was not accepted. Just because I have new information that challenges that conditioning doesn't automatically erase the conditioned response.

What I have learned is that the issue is not that you have bias or an "everyone else," but rather, it is what you do with it once you know you have it. We all have biases and will never be 100 percent free from them, but that should not stop us from consistently growing and improving. This growth is the Inclusive Mindset. Now, whenever I see a Black woman in a romantic relationship with a white man and that conditioned response comes up, I begin to challenge it by creating stories in my head about how they met. The more lavish the story, the better. Sometimes I think they probably were strangers out for a walk, and the wind blew two roses that they each caught in their teeth, and it was at that very moment they locked eyes and knew they would be together forever (I know, I should write romance novels). I also am more intentional about hearing the actual stories of how they met and fell in love.

I created this tactic to challenge my own bias. Intentionally challenging my conditioned negative response into a positive one helps me begin seeing these types of relationships as positive ones. Vernā Myers's TED Talk "How to Overcome Our Biases" deals directly with this as she shows positive images of Black men to begin retraining how we see them.[4] While this tactic of creating positive stories works for me, it can also be helpful to look at positive media coverage of your areas of bias.[5]

UNCOVERING UNCONSCIOUS BIAS

Sometimes we know we are biased and sometimes we don't. There has been a lot of discussion lately on unconscious or implicit bias, and many companies are engaged in extensive training on this. Simply Psychology explains implicit bias this way:

> Implicit bias refers to attitudes or stereotypes that affect our understanding, actions, and decisions in an unconscious way, making them difficult to control. . . . Implicit bias (also called unconscious bias) refers to attitudes and beliefs that occur outside of our conscious awareness and control. Implicit biases are an example of system 1 thinking, such that we are not even aware that they exist. An implicit bias may run counter to a person's conscious beliefs without them realizing it. For example, it is possible to express explicit liking of a certain social group or approval of a certain action, while simultaneously being biased against that group or action on an unconscious level.[6]

The opposite of unconscious or implicit bias is conscious or explicit bias, which are biases you know you have. Many times our unconscious biases are not intentional or malicious, but they are a part of everyday life that need to be challenged. There have been countless studies done on bias, but one that continues to stand out is a study of minorities who altered their résumés when applying for jobs. In the study the minority job applicants sent applications with their experience or activities and reduced any references to their race in hopes of "whitening" their résumés (while all the other experience and details were identical).

The authors of the study shared, "In fact, companies are more than twice as likely to call minority applicants for interviews if they submit whitened resumes than candidates who reveal their race—and this discriminatory practice is just as strong for businesses that claim to value diversity as those that don't."[7] They also found that "twenty-five percent of Black candidates received callbacks from their whitened resumes, while only 10 percent got calls when they left ethnic details intact. Among Asians, 21 percent got calls if they used whitened resumes, whereas only 11.5 percent heard back if they sent resumes with racial references."[8] I don't believe if you asked the recruiters or employers reviewing the applications whether they were intentionally trying to keep these minority candidates out that they would say yes. This is why it is essential for us to continue to understand our biases and how they impact what we do.

Johns Hopkins conducted a study to explore choice and bias with infants and soft colorful blocks. They gave the infants two blocks to choose from, and then after the babies randomly chose one block and played with it, they took the block away and presented them with the "rejected" block and a new block. The babies consistently chose the new block over the block they had previously not chosen. The researchers concluded that maybe what we like is simply based on what we choose.

Think about it this way: when a person makes a decision to choose a political party, a house, or even a haircut (I am bald, so

I don't have that problem), they are making a conscious effort to not pick something else. I call this the difference as wrong versus the difference as different phenomenon. When we pick a position on a topic, we sometimes see an opposing position as wrong versus understanding the specific nuances that might accompany that position. In the study on infants and colorful block choices, Johns Hopkins researchers concluded, "People assume they choose things that they like. But research suggests that's sometimes backwards: We like things because we choose them. And, we dislike things that we don't choose."[9]

Based on this research, it could be that the only reason we do not like certain things, people, or ideas is because we have actively chosen to limit our circles versus expanding our circles. When you operate within the Inclusive Mindset, you actively look for ways to "choose" or engage things that you normally wouldn't, in order to continue growing, learning, and developing; because sometimes the stories we are creating about situations and people are wrong.

LIFE IS MESSY; PEOPLE ARE MESSIER

Have you ever created a story in your mind about someone that you later found out was not true or was more nuanced than you thought? One of my fellow researchers and speakers once shared about a time when he was speaking at a college and it did not appear that the students were paying attention. One student in particular wouldn't get off his phone, which my friend found very disrespectful. He concluded that this student didn't want to be there, and he almost asked him to leave. After the presentation, students came up to talk to him, and the student he was convinced was the worst audience member ever approached and thanked him and then proceeded to show him the many pages of notes he had taken on his phone. My friend was floored and humbled, and it challenged his perspective of people on their phones during his presentations. It also informed my own perspective. Life is messy and people are messier, because we often create narratives for people or situations that aren't always true. Let me share a few examples I have heard from my audience members (who were paying attention).

A Middle Eastern Man on a Plane

After one of my presentations, a guy came up to me and shared a story of his "everyone else." He told me that had a similar experience to the one I had on the plane. He began to tell me of a man he thought was of Middle Eastern descent but was wearing a traditional Western business suit. This gentleman was sitting across the aisle from him, and he noticed the man would not get off his phone, even after the announcement to shut off all electronics came over the intercom. He began to think the worst, that this man may have been plotting to crash the plane into a building, and that was why he was on his phone. He nervously watched this man until the gentleman finally put down his phone when the plane was taking off.

Throughout the flight he continued to watch this man just to make sure things were okay. It did not appear that the turbulence they were experiencing had anything to do with this man, but he continued to stay on guard. When the flight landed he looked over and noticed this man was rushing to grab his stuff, and as soon as the seat belt light went off he ran to the front of the plane and got off in haste. The man shared that he then thought, *Why is that guy so important that he had to get off so fast?* He checked to make sure the gentleman did not leave anything, and as he was looking the pilot came on the intercom system thanking everyone for flying with them and apologizing for the turbulence. The pilot shared, "I am so glad we landed safely, because the gentleman you saw who had to run off the plane when we landed was a doctor who had a heart for someone who was about to die. So hopefully we were able to help in saving someone's life today."

The guy sharing this story talked about how humbled he was at realizing that the reason the doctor wouldn't get off his phone was likely because he was communicating with transportation so that when he landed he could be rushed to the hospital. It is amazing the stories we create about people without even talking to them, but that makes sense because *life is messy and people are messier.*

The Drug Dealer

I was leading a workshop on the Inclusive Mindset a few years back, and as is customary for me I asked the audience to share examples of their "everyone else." One woman spoke up saying that drug dealers were her everyone else. (What mental image did you just have of what a drug dealer looks like?) I shared with her that I understood, that it made perfect sense, and that life was messy and people were messier. Before I could share a story with the audience, another lady chimed in and asked the question, "I wonder who you all thought of when she said drug dealer." I nodded my head in understanding, and she proceeded to share more. She shared that her son (who was white) was a current drug addict and that his drug dealer had been his football coach (who was also white). Her son had a gruesome football injury, and his coach gave him pain pills and told him to not tell his parents. Those consistent illegal pills were the gateway drug for this woman's son. *Life is messy; people are messier.*

Getting Cut Off in Traffic

Have you ever been cut off in traffic? How did you feel? Did you have choice words or maybe even a choice finger (the pinky finger, right?). I remember hearing the story of a really good friend whose twenty-nine-year-old wife's cancer had returned and they were headed to the hospital for an appointment. They walked down the stairs of their building, he opened the door for her, and she got in the car. As they headed to the hospital her body went lifeless. He frantically rushed to the emergency room and parked crookedly as he ran, with his wife's body in his arms, into the emergency room yelling for someone to please save his wife. As I processed that story over and over again, I thought of how many people he had probably cut off on the drive. How many people thought he was being a complete jerk? How many people gave him their "pinky" finger in anger? The stories that we often create about people and situations are pretty interesting, because *life is messy, and people are messier.*

Sex-Offender Registry

I asked this group of attendees at a conference who their "everyone else" was and a lady boldly said to us, "People who are on the sex-offender registry." I shared her concern and concluded that was a really hard one, but life is messy, and people are messier. I thought of a young man's story from many years ago. When he was nineteen years old he was living his life to the fullest. He went to college out of state on a full academic scholarship, and he only went back home for the summer to work a pretty cool internship. One day he met this amazingly beautiful young lady at the grocery store, and they exchanged information. They continued to get to know each other, and over time they chose to be intimate. One time they chose to be intimate in a car in a parking lot. The neighbors thought it was a prostitution issue, so they called the police.

The police came and separated him and the young woman and began to interview them. They came back to his car and asked the young man if he knew that this young woman was fifteen years old. The young man was completely shocked, as the young woman had told him when they first met that she was eighteen years old. Still in shock, he told the police how old she told him she was, and the police confirmed that she had told them that she lied to the young man about her age. The police escorted the young woman home, and the young man was free to go (or so he thought). A few weeks later the young man received a letter from the district attorney's office stating that he was being charged with a felony: statutory rape. Again, he shared his shock and his tears of confusion, because after all, the young lady had lied to him about her age.

Although he had a cool internship, he didn't have money to

pay for an attorney, as he didn't come from a wealthy family, so he was assigned a court-appointed attorney. This attorney told him he should plead guilty and at least then he could get little to no prison time and just probation. The young man was scared, because he knew he didn't want to risk jail time, but he also knew that if he pled guilty to the felony charge he would lose his out-of-state scholarship, because while on probation he would no longer be able to leave the state. He would also forever be on the sex-offender registry. He still had no idea what he would do as the court day approached.

He was in the courthouse when he saw a door open and he recognized the woman who entered; it was the young woman's mom. She went straight to the prosecutor's office and told them that they were about to ruin this young man's life over her daughter's lie. It was then and only then that the prosecutor decided to decrease the felony charge to a misdemeanor "aiding in the delinquency of a minor" charge. The young man was extremely relieved. He was one mother away from potentially being the "everyone else" for the woman in my audience.

You know what's even more interesting? That young man was me. I was one mother away from living a completely different life than I do now. While I am thankful I was able to get that charge expunged eight years later, I recognize that had things gone differently, many people never would have asked me what happened. They never would have asked me my story. They would have created a narrative of what I did as they searched the database of sex offenders living near them. People would have simply taken the exit. Past audience members and people in my training sessions have later shared with me that they had similar stories, but without the mom coming in at the last minute to rescue them.

Thank you for allowing me to share this story, as it is always hard to do. Life is messy; people are messier!

I am certainly not saying that every story can be tied with a pretty bow and have some amazing ending, because not all of them do. Some people really are drug dealers, some people really did cut you off for no good reason, and some people commit heinous crimes, but we don't really know if we take the exit on people. One way to check our biases is to treat each person as if you are learning about them for the first time. Ask deeper questions to understand how they arrived at their position, what inspired them, and what led them to make the decisions they did. You never know what you might uncover and who you might add to your Circles of Grace.

ACTION FORWARD

1. Identify your everyone else and consider making strides to enlarge your Circles of Grace.

2. Take the Six-Month Challenge.

3. Consider talking to an existing friend who holds a difference you want to learn about and have a meaningful conversation (if they don't want to talk about it, that's perfectly fine too).

Chapter 6

WELCOMING VS. INVITING™

How to Enlarge
Our Everyday Circles

I t was the summer of 2017, and I was attending my third National
Speakers Association conference in Orlando, Florida. I walked
into the last keynote of the conference and I felt sad. I didn't feel
like I was connecting with people, and people felt very cliquish. If
you know me, you know I normally don't have a problem connecting with people, and when there is a problem, I lean into it. At the

previous year's conference, I was awarded the highest designation of a speaker, the CSP (Certified Speaking Professional). I did all the things you were supposed to do. I took a proactive approach in reaching out to people, I joined one of the leadership teams for one of the speaker groups, and I even joined the editorial team for the association's magazine, but for whatever reason I did not feel like I was connecting. As I walked into that ballroom, getting ready to go sit in the back by myself, I was convinced this was my last conference, and this would be my last year in the NSA.

As I was heading to my seat in the back, a smiling guy dressed very nicely approached me and said, "Your name is Justin, right?" I recognized him as Brian Walter, the president of the National Speakers Association at the time. I was surprised he even remembered my name, but we had interacted a little bit when I was on the editorial team for *Speaker* magazine. He asked me where I was sitting, and when I told I just planned on sitting in the back he invited me to come sit with him in the front. At his table was his lovely wife, the conference organizers, and hall of fame speaker and marketing guru Bruce Turkel. Brian introduced me to everyone, and I had amazing conversations the rest of that session while seeing the conference from a different perspective.

While everyone who paid for the conference was welcome to attend that keynote, I was invited to the table by Brian. Brian didn't see me as some piddly speaker who needed a hug but rather as an up-and-coming speaker he hadn't connected with yet (yes, in a room of over a thousand people). He had no idea that was going to be my last NSA conference, but that one invitation inspired me to remain a member and continue coming back. My experience has never been the same.

WHAT'S THE DIFFERENCE?

What about you? Have you had an experience like that where either you were invited or you invited someone, and it proved to be a pretty special moment for you and/or them? I realized some years back that there was a difference between being welcomed and invited. Being welcomed isn't bad at all. People are genuinely nice, glad you are there, and they will shake your hand, but there is an expectation (consciously or subconsciously) that you will go back to your circles and they will go back to theirs. Inviting is when a person is humble enough to invite you into their circles and humble enough to go into yours.

Imagine you work for an organization and someone makes an announcement that everyone is welcome to their home for an event, but all you have to do is bring wine (or amazing grape juice if you don't drink). You are excited to go to this event, and you show up with wine in hand and you knock on the door. The person opens the door, says it is so good to see you, takes your wine, and then closes the door in front of you while you peer around him, seeing others enjoying themselves inside the house. Yes, I would be mad too. Everyone was welcomed, but you were not invited into the house. There is a difference, and some of it is semantics.

If you have ever struggled with the difference between diversity and inclusion, this is it in its simplest form. The way it is being implemented today (not the way it was originally meant) is that diversity is being welcomed. It is where people are glad you are here and it is genuine. Inclusion is being invited, where you are not only welcome but given the tour, invited to the inner workings of the organization, and at times invited to "tables" you never even knew existed. Diversity says, "I'm glad *you* are here!" Inclusion says, "I'm glad *we* are here together!" Do you see the difference? While I do not believe that throughout history the people who pushed for diversity ever meant it to be practiced as representation only, understanding inclusion (being invited and inviting) is a helpful way to better understand how to practice true diversity in our communities and our workplaces.

In a DIA Global Forum article, Christine Li writes, "'Diversity without inclusion is exclusion' may initially appear to be nothing more than just a hot catchphrase. However, without inclusion, companies may fail to leverage their diverse talent pool, incorporate various perspectives, and involve different approaches, which may result in failure to maximize their success."[1] Inclusion occurs when people feel they can be their best selves at work or in the organization; in exclusion people don't feel valued or respected, and their talents aren't fully leveraged. In organizations this can sometimes look like people not being invited to serve on important committees or boards, people not being invited to social activities where work relationships are enhanced, or people not being given stretch assignments that showcase opportunities for promotion and growth.

INVITING BEHAVIORS

What behaviors communicate to you that you are invited? I love asking this question in my sessions, because the responses are really good. Here are a few of the responses:

- "When people smile."
- "When someone holds the door open for me."
- "When [I am] in a meeting and someone asks me to share my thoughts and contribution because they know I have something of value to add."
- "When people ask me to join them for lunch. I love food!"
- "When I am asked to be on an important assignment or committee."
- "When I am sitting by myself and a group invites me to sit at their table with them."

There are many other inviting behaviors, but I am curious what you identify as inviting others, or simply put, making others feel more included. I remember being at a conference and something was said on the stage that was a microaggression (I'll talk about that more in chapter 7), something to the effect of "as a Black person they were so articulate" (when they did not mention this for any of the other non-Black people). I knew it wasn't intentional, but it still stung a little. At that moment one of my friends, Jess, who is a white woman, reached out and said, "Can you believe that?" and asked how I was doing. This small gesture made me feel like I wasn't alone, like I was seen. I felt included by that simple text.

Being Invite-able

It not only takes great humility to invite others and include them in things they might not normally be privy too, but it also takes great humility to be invite-able. Being invite-able is not waiting by the phone with a sense of desperation for someone to call (that's what I did in high school), but rather being friendly to others. When asked to go to an event or out after work, especially places you wouldn't normally go, consider it and go out a couple of times. Being invite-able means putting yourself in a position where you can be invited, such as joining volunteer teams or, in my example, helping lead an initiative. I meet many people who don't feel included (and many people legitimately aren't included) but don't take on opportunities that could lead to more access and growth. I am in no way, shape, or form putting the onus on underrepresented or marginalized groups to do something special to get people to do what is right. I am instead asking all of us to assess ourselves and ask, "Am I doing what I can to contribute, help, and assist?"

How can you be not just welcoming but also inviting for others? When you notice people who might feel they are on the outside looking in, identify practical ways you can invite them in. Daniel Fajardo is on the Diversity Committee for the customer service center at Toyota Financial Services in Phoenix, Arizona, and he lives out this message. I interviewed him recently and he shared that when he goes to events, he looks for those who might seem like they are not engaged on the "outside" and he connects with them. He said he wants everyone to know, "I see you're here." This is a great example of being inviting in meaningful ways every day.[2]

Becoming a Mentor

One of the best ways to invite others and make them feel included is being a mentor. Mentors' roles are usually to help show others the ropes. Mentors show people the "hidden" code of success in the organization culture and help them avoid pitfalls. I have had some amazing mentors over the course of my career, including people like Jackie Hrabowski, Forest Harper, Carey McKenzie, Mary Hester-Clifton, Stan Long, John Spence, and Matthew Sullivan, to name a few. They were people who took me under their wing and helped me through some pretty tough times.

Being a mentor is an incredible way to be more inviting. Seeking out a mentor is an incredible way to be invite-able. Being mentored, whether outside your organization or inside can imbue a sense of belonging.

BELONGING

When people are invited and feel respected and valued, it leads to a sense of feeling like you belong. There has rightfully been a new focus in the diversity and inclusion space on belonging, which is a very important aspect of creating inclusive workplaces. Some companies have even gone so far as to include "Belonging" in the Executive of Diversity and Inclusion title. Belonging is important not just in people's titles, but in how people feel included in workplaces and communities. Steven Huang, managing director of the software company Culture Amp, says,

> Belonging is defined as the feeling of security and support when there is a sense of acceptance, inclusion, and identity for a member of a certain group or place.
>
> In order for people to feel like they belong, the environment (in this case the workplace) needs to be set up to be a diverse and inclusive place. Diversity in the workplace is about the mix of different people at a company, whereas inclusion deals with whether or not people feel a sense of

belonging, feel heard, and have a safe space to express themselves authentically.[3]

He shows us how all of these terms really flow and fit together. Belonging is not just some froufrou term, but it does foster some very positive things. Dr. Karyn Hall states, "A sense of belonging to a greater community improves your motivation, health, and happiness."[4] One way to foster a sense of belonging for others is to stand up when we see wrongs, discrimination, or unfair treatment occurring.

GET UP, STAND UP (HAND UP)

In an effort to help people cultivate an Inclusive Mindset, I challenge them not just to think about diversity and inclusion differently but also to feel diversity and inclusion in a different way. One such activity I do is called Get Up, Stand Up (Hand Up). (I include Hand Up for those who are unable to stand.) When I do this virtually, I simply ask people to type their responses to me in the chat. I ask a series of questions about scenarios that have impacted them over the course of their lives, and I am going to ask you a few of those questions. You are welcome to get up and stand up (or put your hand up) if you want; you can circle the phrase or write yes next to it if it rings true; or you can internally reflect on your answer. It's your choice. Here are the questions (in no particular order of importance), and I want you to answer them as it pertains to the course of your whole life.

Have you ever been . . .

- called fat?
- called too skinny?
- called a dumb blond?
- called a dumb jock?
- called an ethnic slur?

- discriminated against because of your gender?
- called a nerd (before it became cool)?
- discriminated against because of your sexuality or identity?
- discriminated against because of your age?
- talked about negatively because either you or your parents did not grow up in this country?
- joked about because you did not have a lot of money?
- falsely perceived to live a perfect life because you grew up with money?
- made to feel less than because you grew up with or still have a disability?
- talked about negatively because of your religion or lack thereof?
- made to feel dumb because of your accent or the way you speak?
- made to feel less than because you have struggled with a mental health issue?
- discriminated against because of your race?
- talked negatively about because you didn't graduate from high school and/or college?
- joked about because you did not grow up in the perceived traditional family structure?
- made to feel less than because you did not work outside of the home?

Or did you hear anything else at some point in your life that hurt or did not make you feel good? I want you to really remember how you felt at that moment. Experience the hurt, disappointment, and frustration. I can probably say that most of us have experienced some form of being "othered," where we were ridiculed, chastised, joked about, or made to feel less than. So why in the world would we ever want anyone else to feel the way we did?

We invite people and make them feel included when we stand up for them, even when they can't stand up for themselves at that moment. When jokes are made, what do we do? When we see unfair treatment occurring, what do we do? I remember a time after I graduated college when I was playing a game with a group of friends, and one of my mentors at the time (unnamed) started joking about those who were different from us. There have been plenty of opportunities where I was a coward and did not speak up. There were other opportunities where I was worse than a coward and joined in. But for whatever reason, this time I decided to say something. I said, "Hey, y'all, we shouldn't be talking about them like that." How do you think they responded? They told me to sit down and shut up, and then they insisted they were just joking. I remember saying, "But if they were joking about us like that, we wouldn't like it." I think I finally summoned the courage to confront wrong because I remembered how it felt to be bullied and talked about negatively, and that feeling inspired me to do something for others. Are you willing to do the same? Because that is operating with an Inclusive Mindset.

You are operating with an Inclusive Mindset when you can get up and stand up for the needs of others, even when it has nothing to do with you. Remember, standing up for people doesn't have to mean that you agree with them, their beliefs, or their choices, but rather you are standing up for their humanity! You are standing up for what is right and good! In organizations this may mean speaking up for those who are being harassed or discriminated against. It could mean noticing who is not at the leadership table and identifying ways to stand up for those groups of people so that they feel more included. After all, wouldn't you want that done for you?

Jess Pettitt and the Invitation

Jess, who identifies as a white queer woman, grew up unpopular because "I just wasn't that cool." She was often the butt of jokes, so she learned to beat people to the punch line. Jess is an inviter. No matter who she is talking to (or bumping into), she invites others in, not because they agree with her, but because inviting is a choice. When I spoke with Jess in 2020, she said, "Inclusion is about actual relationships. . . . Someone who is currently frustrating us now . . . might be the puzzle piece for us later." Jess says that to be an invitation you have to learn to invite yourself too. As the author of *Good Enough Now*, she believes that no matter where you are, you are good enough now to be treated with dignity and to show it to others.[5]

THE TWO RULES

What is the Golden Rule? Do to others what you would want done to you. I think the Golden Rule is amazing, awesome, and powerful. There are even commercials and advertisements that feature it. I love this rule, but what is the Platinum Rule? I love asking this question in my sessions because people come up with some pretty cool responses, like "treat other people better," "respect the mess out of people," and "love people because you have been loved!" I think these are amazing, but let's call them the Bronze Rules. The Platinum Rule is to treat other people the way they want to be treated. Do you know why this is so powerful? Because not everyone wants to be treated the way you treat yourself.

Let's take some practical things like thank-you notes. Some people would prefer a handwritten thank-you note over applause on the video conference or at your next team meeting. Some people walk around like heat-seeking missiles trying to find people to hug, and people who hate to hug run away from them. Imagine you are a person who loves to hug, and you come up to a person who hates to hug, and you say, "Hug the bear!" They are going to run from you and not like it, because that is not how they prefer to be treated. How do we find out how people want to be treated? We ask them. We hear their stories and recognize the significance of each story, which we will cover in chapter 8.

We can choose to operate by the Inclusive Mindset by being not just welcoming to people but also inviting. Let's create a world where we stand up for people being treated unfairly, and let's choose to value people even when we disagree. Let's keep enlarging our circles even when we know we might do or say something stupid.

ACTION FORWARD

1. What is one inviting behavior you can engage in this week? Put it on your calendar so you don't forget.

2. When is the last time you felt invited (included), and what made you feel that way? How can you do that for others?

3. Which of the Get Up, Stand Up (Hand Up) identities resonated the most with you? Why?

Chapter 7

STUPID STUFF
SMART PEOPLE SAY

Understanding the Importance
of Both Intent and Impact

In the summer of 2010, I attended a speaker retreat of sorts. I had just been invited to be part of a speaker's agency, though I wondered why they'd selected me, because there were some heavy hitters in this group, people who were already nationally known or had been on television, as well as speakers I looked up to in the industry. One of the requirements of attending as a new speaker was that I had to speak for seven to ten minutes at the retreat.

When I spoke, I wanted to impress everyone with my relevant research and high energy. When I finished, people stood in line to tell me how good a job I had done (I think they were just being nice). The last person who waited to talk to me was Cindy Pierce. Cindy congratulated me and told me what a great job I had done, but then she asked me a question that would alter my life. She said, "Justin, do mind if I give you some constructive feedback?" I replied, "Of course I don't mind. I want to get better, grow, and develop." She then proceeded to share that several times during my presentation I referred to men as men but to women as girls. In addressing my demeaning communication, she said, "I know that probably wasn't your intent, but I want you to know how that can come across." Wow! I didn't know how to respond, but I profusely apologized because I didn't even realize I was communicating in a demeaning manner. It hit my heart so deeply that when I am in groups of men (or not) and someone else does the same thing, I politely jump in or talk to them later and point it out.

What amazed me the most in the exchange with Cindy was how she handled the conversation. What were the two things Cindy did? First, she asked if she could give me feedback. Second, she assumed I had a positive intent. She did not come to me yelling, "You misogynist pig! You hate the very womb that bore you!" Let me tell you a secret. If you ever want someone's defensive walls to come up fast, don't ask to give them feedback and always assume they meant the absolute worst. It was Cindy's approach that really taught me about intent and impact and why both are important.

IMPORTANCE OF BOTH INTENT AND IMPACT

Have you ever said or done something stupid? If you have, simply nod with me (don't hurt your neck now). For those who didn't nod your head, you just did something stupid, because all of us have done or said some pretty stupid stuff at times. I know I have . . . ask my kids. I learned a few important things from my interaction with Cindy. I realized that I could have a negative impact even if my intentions were good. And the reverse is also true: just because a person is impacted negatively doesn't mean that the other person had bad intentions. Each person needs to approach the other person, receive feedback, and deliver feedback with a level of humility.

To be clear, good intentions don't excuse or minimize negative impact or avoid potential consequences. However, I do believe that we should ultimately treat others who have done or said something wrong the way we would want to be treated when we have done or said something wrong. *We tend to judge ourselves by our intent, while we judge others by their impact.* Have you noticed that when we inadvertently offend someone, we say, "That's not what I meant," but when someone does something that upsets us, we say, "Don't you know how that made me feel?" Both intent and impact are important to consider as we seek to grow in an Inclusive Mindset.

Intent and Impact Examples

I have created four different scenarios to look at the results of a conversation based on intent and impact.

Scenario 1: Positive Intent and Positive Impact

This is the best-case scenario, as someone says something with a positive intent and it is received positively. This could be when someone says something like "I really like how you led the meeting today. You showed clear thought, wisdom, and strategic direction. Thank you!" Words were meant well and received well.

Action
- ▸ Receiver of statement: Sincerely thank the person for the compliment and encouragement. Maybe ask what specific actions they noticed as you led the meeting.
- ▸ Giver of statement: Nothing. You've done enough good for the day.

Scenario 2: Positive Intent and Negative Impact

This is one of the more challenging scenarios. Someone might say, "Wow, you speak pretty clearly for a Southerner." Now, you might be defensive right now if you are a Southerner, but many times people have been exposed to negative stereotypes with people who have a Southern drawl or speak with a Southern accent. They might not know any better, though that doesn't excuse what they said.

Action

▶ Receiver of statement: Ask deeper questions like "What do you mean by that?" or "Tell me more, because most of the Southerners I know who speak with an accent speak pretty clearly." Of course, try your best to ask the question without projecting a negative attitude toward the person you're talking to. Ask to give them feedback and let them know that you aren't questioning their intentions; you just want to help them.

▶ Giver of statement: Don't get defensive. Apologize and realize that you made a mistake. Own up to it and take it as a learning opportunity to communicate better next time. Also check to see if you might have an implicit bias toward Southerners who speak with a Southern accent or drawl.

Scenario 3: Negative Intent and Negative Impact

This is the worse-case scenario, as the giver not only meant harm, but the other person received the statement as hurtful. A person might nastily say, "I believe the world was a better place when women stayed at home and did womanly duties."

Action

▶ Receiver of statement: I know you want to react, but don't. Ask, "What do you mean by that?" Based on the answer you can choose not to respond or say something like, "There are many families where one person stays home and it works well for them, but I am glad my partner and I agree that a woman's contributions aren't just for the household but for society as a whole."

▶ Giver of statement: First of all, what are you trying to accomplish with this nasty remark? Please acknowledge your error, apologize for your actions, and educate yourself on the benefits of women in the workplace, even if you and your partner chose differently. Just because something is different doesn't mean it's wrong.

Scenario 4: Negative Intent and Positive Impact

This was the hardest scenario to provide an example for, as this is more about how the receiver takes a comment. A millennial might say something like "I didn't think that as an old person you could still adapt to a competitive company like ours."

Action

▶ Receiver of statement: This is a toss-up, because you can either ignore the comment or ask, "What do you mean by that?" Or you could share something like "In my many years on this earth, I have had to adapt to a lot, and so my age really is a competitive advantage because I've been able to apply that to this organization."

▶ Giver of statement: Again, what are you trying to accomplish with your negative intentions? Please acknowledge your error and focus instead on the accomplishments and contributions that another generation brings to the team or company. Please apologize.

While every situation will be different and should be handled differently, it is important to be humble no matter what position you are in or what side of the conversation you are on. If you are the receiver of the statement, challenge your automatic response to be offended. You may choose instead to respond with curiosity, such as "Tell me more" or "What did you mean by that?" If you are the giver of the statement, acknowledge your error and think about times when you may have been in the other person's position and were offended by what someone said to you. If you had good intent, take what that person said seriously. It doesn't always mean you need to change what you believe or are doing (I have been given some horrible feedback over the years), but allow it to be a strong data point for you to consider shifting how you communicate or what you do. You may be tempted to get defensive, because we never like feeling that we did something wrong, but with an Inclusive Mindset we look for ways to grow in matters of diversity and inclusion. When you mess up or make a mistake, how do you see yourself? Do you see it as an action of failing or an identity of being a failure? Failure at times can be extremely painful, but it does not have to be final, as we can learn and grow from it.

But What If They Meant It?

I hear you loud and clear . . . "How should I respond if I'm 99.9 percent sure they meant it in a negative way?" First, the truth is you really never know what people mean unless you ask them, and second, it can be helpful to defuse the situation with kindness when someone is intentionally trying to be mean. As Michelle Obama says, "When they go low, you go high!"

MICROAGGRESSIONS

Sometimes the stupid stuff smart people say is considered a microaggression. Kevin Nadal, a professor of psychology and researcher of microaggression, states, "Microaggressions are defined as the everyday, subtle, intentional—and oftentimes unintentional—interactions or behaviors that communicate some sort of bias toward historically marginalized groups. The difference between microaggressions and overt discrimination or macroaggressions, is that people who commit microaggressions might not even be aware of them."[1] Sometimes microaggressions aren't statements at all but could be something like talking over women in a meeting when you don't do that to men, or referring to a group of people as "you people." Medical News Today shares three different types of microaggressions:[2]

1. **Microassaults.** These are commonly described as "old-fashioned racism" because the person behaves deliberately in a discriminatory manner. However, they are not intending to offend someone or may not think their actions are harmful. The person will not openly say they are acting in a discriminatory way.
2. **Microinsults.** These occur when people unintentionally or unconsciously say discriminatory things or behave in a discriminatory way. When people communicate microinsults, they may believe that they are complimenting the person. However, they are actually making insulting statements.
3. **Microinvalidations.** These are actions and behaviors that deny racism and discrimination. Invalidations occur when a person undermines the struggles of target groups. Racism is present in society, and people who believe it does not exist negate reality.

Microaggressions are harmful to the recipients and can lead to anxiety, depression, and other mental health challenges, as well as decreased productivity and job satisfaction. However, more often than not they are not meant in a harmful manner, even if they come across as pretty stupid.

I know I have said some stupid stuff in my life. What about you? Here are some examples of common stupid stuff smart people say:

- Speaking to a person with a Southern accent: "I didn't realize you were so smart."
- Speaking to a woman: "How does your husband feel about you working?"
- Speaking to an Asian American: "You speak really good English."
- Speaking to a Black person: "Wow, I didn't expect you to be so articulate."
- Speaking to an older person: "I know technology may be hard for you."
- Speaking to a Black woman: "I didn't expect you to have really *good* hair."

What are some examples of stupid stuff you've heard or maybe said yourself? Even more important, what can you do to help stop or mitigate microaggressions when they happen? If they happen to someone else, stand up for the other person and address it. Oftentimes we believe the person who has been wronged needs to address the wrong, but we need more people standing up for others (see chapter 11).

If you experience a microaggression, address it if it is worth your time, energy, and mental space. Sometimes it may just be enough to vent to a person you trust, and sometimes you need to address the offender head-on. When addressing the slight, please be mindful that this person may have no idea they did anything wrong, and how you approach them might lead to defensiveness. While you can't control how someone responds, you can create an environment where your input will be more welcome, which will hopefully lead to a meaningful conversation and better understanding. While change may not always occur immediately, you may have planted a very valuable seed in that person's future growth, even if you never see it.

Jeremy Poincenot: Golfing and Sight

For the first nineteen years of Jeremy's life, he was fully sighted, but when he was a sophomore in college, he rapidly lost his central vision, rendering him legally blind. He recalled the fear, the challenges, and the stupid stuff people would say and do. He said he is all in for blind jokes now (as long as they are tasteful), but when he first lost his sight he wasn't. People wonder all the time how he has become a blind golf champion, and they have a lot of questions. In our interview he shared some tips on how to approach conversations with those who are different *and minimize the stupid stuff we say and do.* He shared that you have to approach conversations with people with genuine caring. He said, "I can almost always tell people's true intentions."

He also gave some really good tips for engaging those who are disabled (some people say differently abled). He said, "You can never go wrong by asking. . . . I would always rather be asked something than someone assuming I can't do it." He said that the first step to accommodating someone is asking, not assuming. Jeremy encourages people to step out of their comfort zone and ask one or two questions they would not normally ask when engaging someone who is different. Fortunately, he also gave some great advice regarding when you say or do the wrong thing when you have good intentions. He encourages people to own it and apologize sincerely even though "I'm sorry isn't the magic wand." He challenges people to not deflect or bounce from the situation but hash it out and come to common ground if you are able. I agreed with Jeremy when he said, "At the end of the day we are all people!" Let's choose to engage people with curiosity and wonder.[3]

ACTION FORWARD

1. Identify a time when you had good intentions, but your actions had a negative impact on someone else. How did you react when confronted?

2. Identify a time when you experienced a negative impact, but you believed the person had good intentions. How did you react?

3. What is one microaggression you have said/done that you will work to stop using/doing?

Chapter 8

THE KID ON THE PLANE WHO WOULDN'T SHUT UP

Rediscovering Courageous Curiosity and Authentic Listening

I was getting ready for a nine-day, eight-city speaking tour. I had slept for only two hours, as I may have been up all night watching *Frozen*. (Don't judge me. I have young kids.) I was excited to get on that plane and fall asleep on the way to my first layover. I boarded the plane and as I began to sit down in my aisle seat, I saw this little kid, who was about eight years old, sitting in the window

85

seat in my row. It appeared this little kid was flying alone, as he had one of those "don't mess with me because I am flying alone" things around his neck. I immediately sat down, hoping to be left alone and fall asleep before takeoff. It wasn't ten seconds into my pretend sleep that this little kid started yapping.

He started talking to the lady in between us, whom I believe was from the country of Laos. I was slowly (well, maybe quickly) getting upset because I wanted to sleep, and I had forgotten my Bose noise-cancelling headphones. So I did what any person would have done at that moment . . . I listened. And when I did, I discovered this little kid was doing two pretty amazing things. He was engaged in courageous curiosity and authentic listening. He was asking the woman questions like, "What is Laos like?" and "What should I know?" and "What do you plan on doing while you are here in the States?" He not only asked some incredible questions, but he also followed up with more really good questions that were based on his great listening. I learned so much about effective communication from that kid on the plane that I share it with others around the world.

COURAGEOUS CURIOSITY

What is the number-one question kids ask? No, it is not "Are we there yet?" but rather "Why? Why? Why?" The never-ending barrage of "Why?" screams curiosity (which you can tell I like based on the title of my last book, *Your Why Matters Now*), but it can also be annoying. When we were this little kid's age, we knew nothing, so we asked questions because we were framing the world around us. When we get older, we ask questions like we know everything (if we ask them at all), and we only know slightly more. I think it's time we go back to our little kid selves and approach the world and the people in it with wonderment and curiosity.

One way to approach the world in this way is to first acknowledge that everyone has a story, and each story has significance. We should listen to one of the greatest philosophers of the last hundred years (Kendrick Lamar), who told us to "sit down [and] be humble," because it takes great humility to seek to be more interested than interesting. I have noticed that more people focus on trying to impress others than they do on getting to know the person they are talking to. This is one of the reasons I have loathed going to "networking" events. People typically go to find someone who can do something for them (transactional relationships), or they are going to show how amazing they are. While most people ask the two questions "What do you do?" and "Where do you work?" I like to ask, "What are you the most passionate about?" and "What are you interested in learning (non-work related) that you haven't learned before?"

Which kind of person are you? If you realize that you often are more focused on sharing who you are, your perspective, and your views when meeting people, perhaps you might consider becoming more curious about others.

Researchers Celeste Kidd and Benjamin Hayden describe curiosity this way:

> The most popular theory about the function of curiosity is to motivate learning. George Loewenstein [1994] described curiosity as "a cognitive induced deprivation that arises from the perception of a gap in knowledge and understanding." Loewenstein's information gap theory holds that curiosity functions like other drive states, such as hunger, which motivates eating. Building on this theory, Loewenstein suggests that a small amount of information serves as a priming dose, which greatly increases curiosity.[1]

That is a fancy way of saying that the best way to grow in your curiosity is to start learning. In a 2009 study by Min Jeong Kang and colleagues, they associated curiosity with an inverted U-shape. They found that people had the least amount of curiosity when they knew nothing about the topic *and* when they felt extremely confident about their knowledge on said topic. The people who were the most curious were somewhere in the middle between having no clue and having great confidence.[2]

This is where the courage part kicks in. First, it takes courage to ask other people about themselves and risk rejection, because people either don't want to talk or don't want to talk right now. Second, it takes courage to just get started, because if you are unknowledgeable, especially about a matter of diversity and inclusion, you may have less motivation to learn about someone or something unfamiliar. Your level of curiosity might start off low . . . until you start learning, and over time your curiosity will likely grow. The best way to grow in courageous curiosity is to simply start and take the first step in your learning journey. Identify one specific question that you want answered and dive in.

For example, if a person wanted to better understand some of the issues surrounding gender equity in the workplace, they may start with learning about the widely known topic of pay gaps or talking to a female colleague about her experiences within the organization. If a person wanted to learn about racism, they might start by researching racism as it pertains to the criminal justice system and watch a documentary like *13th*. If a person wanted to learn about millennials, they might watch many of the TED Talks about them, like one by Reniqua Allen.[3] We have never lived at a time when there is so much rich information around us, but the richest of information sometimes lies within the people we interact with on a daily basis. The Inclusive Mindset is all about stimulating a daily curiosity in things and others, and when we are curious, we must listen.

AUTHENTIC LISTENING

I continue to marvel at how that kid on the plane listened to the lady next to him. He was performing a master class on how to listen. He engaged in what I call authentic listening, because I have learned you can fake active listening (I used to teach it).

All you have to do is (1) repeat what the person just said to you, (2) mimic their behaviors, and (3) lean in to show them you are really interested—that gets them every time. Those three things don't communicate real listening, and real active listening is authentic listening by another name. Real active listening is defined as

> the ability to focus completely on a speaker, understand their message, comprehend the information and respond thoughtfully. Unlike passive listening, which is the act of hearing a speaker without retaining their message, this highly valued interpersonal communication skill ensures you're able to engage and later recall specific details without needing information repeated.[4]

Authentic listening is completely losing yourself in the conversation with that person, to the point where you might forget what you wanted to say because you are listening that intently.

You know when people are really listening to you. They may or may not make eye contact, but they are focused on you. They have amazing follow-up questions that convey what you just shared and point to something deeper that you might not have said yet. Authentic listening is not an act but rather a state of being.

The Research

A study published by *Harvard Business Review* found four characteristics of authentic listening: (1) Listening is not being silent and letting the other speak but rather having a dialogue and asking insightful questions that draw out more insights. (2) Good listening is a positive experience that is not overly critical but rather instills confidence. (3) Good listening is more cooperative than combative. Good listening isn't paying attention to find the errors in what the person is sharing, and it is certainly not about trying to win an argument. (4) Good listeners offer suggestions, though not immediately. After the person feels like they have been heard, realistic suggestions can be offered.[5] Research has also shown that the older we get the less efficient we are in listening, but at the same time the better we think we are at listening.[6] We may think we know what the person is saying, or we may use our own historical references to filter what the person is saying, without really listening to them. It's time for us to learn how to be better listeners and become more like that little kid on the plane.

Become the Little Kid

That little kid inspired me so much that I became like him and wouldn't shut up on my next flight. I was sitting next to a gentleman, and we discussed a major controversial topic in our society at the time. We disagreed, but we were both genuinely curious about the other's position and how we came to that conclusion. When we landed, we did not walk off the plane singing "We Are Family" and we still did not agree, but we set up a lunch meeting to further discuss the issue.

One amazing thing that remains constant is that people still generally enjoy talking about themselves. Study after study confirms this predictable phenomenon that talking about ourselves (or self-disclosure) is physiologically rewarding.[7] When people start talking about themselves, they share a little part of their lives with you. They are genuinely interested in sharing the significance of their stories as they recall past experiences. That is why hearing other people's stories is so vital, because it is a gateway into meaningful conversations. While there are always exceptions to the rule, most people are willing to share their stories if they feel the other person is trustworthy and curious for reasons that won't hurt them in the future. It's time we better engage in the number-one thing that people like to talk about: themselves.

Double-Dutch Communication

Unfortunately, most people communicate in what I call a double-Dutch style. Oh, you don't know what double Dutch is? It is a form of jumping rope. Jumping rope is normally done with a single rope, but double Dutch is using two ropes, and someone is off to the side moving front to back, waiting for the perfect opportunity to jump in. That is how we often communicate with others: we are looking for the moment when we can jump into the conversation to share why we disagree. We are waiting for them to take a breath, pause, or think for a second so we can jump in. This method of communication is completely ineffective and does not convey listening to understand. One way to get out of this mode of communicating is the Power of Three.

The Power of Three™

The Power of Three is simply listening to the third level of the conversation. What I have found is that most people listen to the Power of One or the Power of Two.

Power of One:

Person A: How are you doing today?
Person B: I'm doing great!
Person A: I remember last week when I was doing great . . .

Power of Two:

Person A: How are you doing today?
Person B: I'm doing great!
Person A: What made you great?
Person B: I had an amazing walk with my kids!
Person A: When I went on a walk with my kids, it was pure joy and we talked about . . .

Power of Three:

Person A: How are you doing today?
Person B: I'm doing great!
Person A: What made you great?
Person B: I had an amazing walk with my kids!

Person A: What did you enjoy the most about your walk?
Person B: The conversation was so rich, and I learned so
many things.

Do you see the difference in the examples other than their length? Many people cannot wait to get the conversation back to themselves, and that's exactly what they do. What if when you engage with people you listen at least to the Power of Three? I am not saying you just let the other person talk (which has actually been shown as a negative in effective listening), but actively engage them in the conversation. I am also not saying don't talk about yourself ever (after all, science shows you like to), but first get to something meaningful in the conversation about the person you are talking to and then share something about yourself that connects with that meaningful point.

When we operate by the Inclusive Mindset, we listen deeply to others to better understand them. This takes intentionality at first if you are not used to having a conversation this way, and then over time it becomes a little more natural.

"Tell Me More" and Other Powerful Questions

One powerful thing I often say is "Tell me more." I have found that most people stop sharing prematurely because they think most people don't really care (we all have that one friend who challenges this truth . . . is it you?). I have found that "tell me more" gives people permission to keep going, letting them know you actually want to know more about them or their stories. Other ways to phrase this could be "Can you share more about your experience?" or "What was your favorite part about that?" In a workplace a few powerful questions are "What do you think?" and "Why?" You don't want to be robotic with this, as you want to flow with the conversation, but by all means ask questions.

We don't ask enough questions, and we don't ask questions that people would love to answer. In studying conversations, Alison

Wood Brooks and Leslie John found that "people don't ask enough questions. In fact, among the most common complaints people make after having a conversation, such as an interview, a first date, or a work meeting, is 'I wish [s/he] had asked me more questions' and 'I can't believe [s/he] didn't ask me any questions.'"[8] In their research for the article "The Surprising Power of Questions," they found four types of questions and that:

> Not all questions are created equal. Alison's research, using human coding and machine learning, revealed four types of questions: introductory questions ("How are you?"), mirror questions ("I'm fine. How are you?"), full-switch questions (ones that change the topic entirely), and follow-up questions (ones that solicit more information). Although each type is abundant in natural conversation, follow-up questions seem to have special power. They signal to your conversation partner that you are listening, care, and want to know more. People interacting with a partner who asks lots of follow-up questions tend to feel respected and heard.[9]

Question asking is not an interrogation but a part of the beauty of meaningful conversation, so your focus should be not on how many questions you can ask but how many really good questions you can ask. There is a certain magic in a conversation that is catalyzed by good questions.

ACTION FORWARD

1. Identify one person you can be courageously curious with this week and put it on your calendar to reach out.

2. What is one area of listening where you can improve? Practice it with the person from question 1.

3. Do you tend to listen to the Power of One or Two when talking to people? Try to listen to the Power of Three and ask one of your friends or family members some power questions.

Chapter 9

DISCOVERING DIALOGUE AND EXERCISING EMPATHY

How to Communicate with Almost Anyone to Better Understand Their Perspective and Position

I sat by myself at the retreat center wondering what I should do. On this retreat with Leadership Charlotte (a nonprofit organization designed to help leaders better serve the city of Charlotte, North Carolina), we were encouraged to dig deep and identify ways in which our past had shaped us. One of the glaring parts of my past was my relationship with my father. My parents divorced when I was around four years old, and I lived with my mom. There was a period of time when my dad traveled two and a half hours every other weekend to pick me up and then drop me off. As I got older that started to slow to one weekend a month, until it stopped altogether. There were several reasons for that, which I'm not going to get into at this time (maybe another book). No matter the reasons, there were stretches where I did not see or talk to my dad for years. I didn't think about it all that much then, but as I got older and especially as I had kids of my own, I realized how much that absence impacted me.

Sitting at this retreat center in the fall I made a decision. I knew I was going to Ghana (where my dad was born, raised, and retired) the next summer, and I decided I would confront him. Ask him the painful questions of why he didn't fight for me and what made it so easy for him not to engage his firstborn son. I was hurt and I was going to let him know that I was hurt. Every time I thought of how I would confront him I got angrier and angrier.

As time went on, my position on how I wanted to approach my dad started to change because of therapy and some amazing wisdom from my Leadership Charlotte cohort. I shifted from going to confront my dad to choosing to hear his story. I wanted to better understand how he grew up and what happened between him and my mom that caused a break in our relationship. I no longer wanted what would have been a monologue; now I desired a dialogue with my dad.

After I arrived in Ghana and my dad and I were finally able to sit down and talk, I asked to hear his story growing up. I asked him what happened, and how it made him feel not to see me for all those years. As he shared his story and perspective, I tried to put myself in his position to better understand his decisions. I began to have more clarity about what happened, and I wasn't angry with my dad anymore, even though I would have made some different choices. I chose to forgive my dad, and I was able to exercise empathy toward him. The dialogue with my dad had positive ripple effects over my life for years to come.

In this chapter you are going to find more lists and more how-tos, as dialogue and empathy are areas most people want to get better in. I have shared multiple ways to practice and live these out in your everyday life.

DIALOGUE DEFINED

So, what is dialogue anyway? Is it just some fancy way to communicate with others? One of the best books I read while I was getting my MBA was *Dialogue and the Art of Thinking Together* by William Isaacs. In that book and subsequent other books, I learned so much about dialogue and its positive impact. Most people treat conversations as debates, not dialogue. We enter into conversations to win them, not to exchange information and ultimately create something new together. Dialogue is not leaving your views and opinions at the door, but it is about approaching your conversations in a more collaborative way.

Isaacs says dialogue "is a conversation with a center, not sides,"[1] and that it "is about a shared inquiry, a way of thinking and reflecting together."[2] It is also "a living experience of inquiry within and between people. . . . The most important parts of any conversation are those that neither party could have imagined before starting."[3] Dialogue is about creating something new together. It is about continuing the conversation and starting from a position that your perspective or viewpoint is not the final word. You are truly open to other possibilities, even if you don't agree with them or fully understand how they got there. To simplify it, dialogue is not about convincing someone of A, nor is it someone else convincing the other party of B; it is creating C together.

Oftentimes we approach conversations as evidence gatherers seeking every point that will prove us right and the other person or idea wrong. Imagine two giant gates and between them is water. Dialogue is like letting down your gates together to relieve the tension of the water, allowing new things to pass by. Dialogue is more than just getting along or having affirming conversations. It gets to the root of the conversation and goes deep while allowing us to still hear, value, and respect other parties. In describing dialogue, William Isaacs states,

> The idea of thinking together can sound like a dangerous illusion in which the quest for harmony leads people astray until they unwittingly sacrifice their individuality. But in assiduously avoiding false harmony, people can go to the other extreme—to an equally unwitting 'argument' mode in which we stand in a stagnated pond of our own predispositions and certainties and blindly defend what we have as necessary and unalterable. In both cases—in false harmony and in polarized, argumentative stagnation—people stop thinking.[4]

Politeness does not always equal dialogue. There are many people who have learned to be polite but are still approaching the conversation like a battle to be won; they just wage war with a smile.

When we engage in dialogue, we approach people and especially those who are different from us with a beginner's mindset. This means we acknowledge and suspend our assumptions and preexisting thoughts about that "type" of person (we'll talk about this more later in the chapter). Are we so full of our own thoughts and views that we do not have room to process other people's views? Are we bursting at the seams with our own thoughts, and the only thing that will relieve us is getting out everything we are thinking versus considering what others are sharing? When we engage people in dialogue, we enter into the conversation as a student—one who is ready and willing to learn and grow from the information and experiences the "teacher" has to share—but it does take a process to get to and stay in dialogue. Dialogue is one essential way to better develop an Inclusive Mindset, and it is well worth the effort to grow in communicating this way.

The Dialogue Process

While there is no one-size-fits-all approach to dialogue, William Isaacs researched and found that there are four practices for dialogue.

1. *Listening*: We should listen to others while we work to quiet our own inner voices that are making assumptions or only hearing people in efforts to prove or disprove their point of view. Listening is not done in silence; it is participatory, not passive.

2. *Respecting*: When you respect someone, you honor them and the experiences that have shaped them and their perspectives. Respecting someone doesn't mean you have to always agree with what they think or do, but you do need to see their humanity. You see the person or perspective having value to give. You see them as a potential teacher you can learn from.

3. *Suspending*: When in a conversation we sometimes start to formulate an opinion, often stemming from unconscious biases we all have. We can choose to defend our view or suspend it temporarily. This is neither accepting the other's perspective nor putting your own perspective down, but rather suspending it (pressing pause) to try to see their perspective with fresh eyes.

4. *Voicing*: This means sharing what is true for you, or as some people put it, speaking your truth. It is saying what we genuinely think and feel, which takes great courage. This is done in a respectful and honoring way, but you still share your authentic voice and don't hold it in.[5]

Tips for Effective Dialogue

There are countless ways to have effective dialogue, but here are some pointers I've found to be helpful.

Choose to dialogue. The first thing we should do is choose to have a dialogue. I know this sounds simple, but oftentimes how we approach conversations is critical. If we approach conversations to win them (which we often do), then that is how we will choose to communicate. But if we go into a conversation saying to ourselves that we want to have a dialogue and really hear the other person's perspective and learn something new, this will help us actually follow through.

Check bias and underlying assumptions. In chapter 5 we talked about not taking the exit, and this is important because often second- and thirdhand information will get in the way of really hearing the other person, because we insist to ourselves that we know what they really mean. One practical way to deal with this is to admit to yourself that you have an underlying assumption or bias. Sometimes in the right situation this can be shared with a person or persons you are communicating with. Another practical thing you can do is acknowledge that your questions may be full of assumptions and change the way you ask questions. In hearing my dad's story, I may have received a different response if I'd asked him, "What made you abandon me?" versus "What happened that we were apart for so long?" This subtle shift has the potential to change the tone and response during conversations.

Separate identity and ideology. You are not your ideas. I was speaking once at a company and the question came up about being fully accepted. This person wanted to know how they could respect someone or listen to someone who didn't fully accept them, their thoughts, and their ideas. We think people need to agree with us 100 percent to fully accept us, and that is because we equate our identity with our ideology. People can fully accept us as human beings without fully accepting what we believe, think, or do. For example, I don't like a lot of things my children do (e.g., sneaking food upstairs, being ungrateful, and angrily telling me they don't like me), but I fully accept them.

Seek opportunities for genuine common ground. Even when

we disagree with others, whatever our reason, it should not prohibit us from being able to learn something new. Constantly ask yourself, "What can I learn?" and "What common ground do we share?" Focusing on these two things allows us to dialogue better with others. I have seen this work well in conversations about small ideas and even really big ideas like gun rights and gun laws.[6]

Embrace your ignorance. Embracing your ignorance means coming to the realization that there may be a lot for you to learn about this area, and the person you are talking to probably has something to teach you. I remember going to a workshop about an area I didn't generally agree with, and before I went I challenged myself by asking, *What can I learn? Because there is a lot I do not know.*

Embracing our ignorance does not mean that we say to ourselves, *I don't know about it and will never know about it, and that's fine with me!* That is more about pride and ego, which can hurt genuine dialogue. Learning something new or hearing a different perspective doesn't mean someone else has "won," but all parties win when we walk away with a new idea or a new perspective. When we come to the table vulnerably and admit that we do not have all the answers, we can have a deeper dialogue and more learning can occur.[7]

Ask questions to listen, not leverage. Do you find yourself asking questions of others, not to really glean something new or better understand, but rather to gather data points so that you can tell them how wrong they are and what they are saying doesn't make sense? We should ask questions to understand, not to trap people. Have you ever met someone who asked a question they knew the answer to, but they were just trying to set you up for what they wanted to say next? Don't be that person, because great questions expose us to thoughts and beliefs we might not have previously encountered. One practical way to do this is to ask yourself, "What more can I learn?" as well as saying things like "Tell me more!"

Keep an open body posture. While there is no absolute right or wrong way to have a dialogue, how you approach someone physically can impact how they perceive if you are listening. If you seem distracted and are checking your phone, it may come off that you aren't listening. If you cross your arms and lean back, you may be communicating that you are hostile to what's being shared. However, if you lean forward and maintain eye contact, you have the potential to communicate that you are open to hearing the other person. How I physically listen to those I disagree with is still a work in progress for me, but knowing what I do is helpful to start trying new ways to physically listen. I now go into conversations more aware of when I cross my arms, and when I do I challenge myself to uncross them and lean forward.

Dialogue takes practice, and just because you might have more knowledge and more tools at your disposal doesn't mean you will always get it right. I certainly still struggle with having productive dialogue; however, I continue to practice and focus on specific areas (e.g., suspending my biases or changing my body posture) when I engage with others. Practice makes progress! Continuing to grow in this area is important because when you are able to engage in deep dialogue, you can truly hear the other person and think with them. This will open the door to feeling someone else's pain and hearing their perspective, which ultimately opens the door to exercising empathy.

EMPATHY EXPLAINED

Empathy has been described in many different ways. *Psychology Today* defines it as "imagining yourself in someone else's skin: feeling what they feel and seeing yourself and the world from their point of view."[8] While some may define it as understanding someone else's feelings and experiences, Sara Konrath, a researcher on empathy, takes it a step further: "Empathy is both imagining other people's perspectives and their world's cognitive type of empathy, and it's also caring, compassion and concern for others, that emotional empathy."[9] There appear to be head and heart levels expressed in empathy, where you engage the other person not only cognitively but also emotionally. Author Justin Bariso organizes empathy into three categories:

Cognitive: I understand how you feel (mentally understanding someone's view and their feelings).

Emotional: I share your feelings (someone is crying, and you start crying).

Compassionate: I'm doing this to help relieve your pain (feeling their pain and taking action to help).[10]

Having empathy for others is a key component of the Inclusive Mindset, as it allows you to better experience the journey of someone else. In a world of conflict and disunity we need more empathy. Empathy helps us engage in "cooperation and unity rather than conflict and isolation."[11] Unfortunately, the very thing that has been essential for unity and minimizing conflict has been eroding over the years. One study conducted over thirty years (1979–2009) analyzing more than fourteen thousand young people showed that people feeling concern for others decreased by 48 percent, and people imagining things from other's perspective decreased by 34 percent.[12] I am afraid of what they might find over the next ten years. It is no wonder things feel more divisive than ever. We are losing the art of being able to feel each other's pain and see each other's perspectives, but the exciting news is that it is something we can improve.

While some researchers have thought that empathy is solely a genetic trait that you are born with or not, further research has shown that it is also something that can be influenced and developed. Like any other skill, we can grow in empathy toward others as long we make the choice to. Making that choice is more critical than ever. If we think we can't be empathetic, we are less likely to engage in empathy, but if we think we can grow and become more empathetic, we increase our likelihood of being empathetic toward others.[13] Having more empathy allows us to better understand others and ultimately grow in the Inclusive Mindset. Empathy allows us to be better leaders, and it allows others to feel heard and seen, even if you may not always agree.

What Empathy Is Not

Empathy is not sympathy ("Wow, I hate that you are going through that"). Empathy is going through it with another person even if you can't fully understand what they are thinking and/or feeling. You will never know 100 percent how someone else feels no matter how hard you try. I will never fully know what it feels like to be a woman in corporate America. No matter how hard I try and no matter the number of books I read, I will never know 100 percent, but that doesn't stop me from better understanding. It is crucial to avoid language like "I know exactly how you feel." Instead, use language like "I better understand what that is like."

Empathy is also not pity. Pity is when you feel sorry for someone. An article in *Psychology Today* shared the differences between what most people think of when they consider empathy. "*Pity:* I acknowledge your suffering; *sympathy:* I care about your suffering; *empathy:* I feel your suffering; *compassion:* I want to relieve your suffering."[14] The latter two are how I define empathy, because what you feel should lead to a desire to do something more.

Empathy is also not agreement. Some people avoid empathy for others because they feel it means tacit approval, but that is untrue. You can be empathetic for someone while not being in agreement with them. You can feel their pain even if you can't understand how they came to feel that pain. Following are a few ways to better exercise empathy with others.

Tips for Exercising Empathy

I remember having trouble with the payment provider for my business. I called to get it solved, and I had four horrible calls. Some people showed me pity (acknowledged my pain), which was likely to have been scripted. Some were just plain rude, as if I had done something to cause the issue I was having. I assure you I did no such thing. I then reached the fifth person, and this fifth person said a few things that struck me. He said, "I really want to help you," "I hate what you are going through," and "I don't want to add to your trouble." He stayed on the phone with me versus sending me to the next person. I felt like he was in it with me, and it made me feel vastly better about my experience. I wish I could say he solved my issue, because no matter how hard he tried he couldn't, but I felt seen and I felt better. What things can you and I do to help people feel seen and feel better? Here are some suggestions:

Take fifteen to thirty minutes to have a meaningful conversation. Each day and/or week take time to meaningfully connect with someone outside of social media. Research has found that social media and its networks are very "me centered," which can negatively impact our empathy toward others. So, we should get off the social media app and consider calling or video-conferencing someone to hear how they are doing, ask about their story, or get their perspective regarding something occurring in society.

Stay curious, my friend. Ask to hear other people's stories or things that have shaped what they now think and/or believe. Ask people to connect you with others who might share a perspective that piqued your interest. Engage with people you don't know. This could be a new organization, neighbors, or people in an identity group that you are interested in learning more about.

Walk a mile. Having conversations is great, but go with people on their journeys. In my Leadership Charlotte cohort, we went through a poverty simulation (I didn't have to simulate because that's how I initially grew up). The simulations showed us how some might experience the city and the unique challenges people might go through to simply live. When engaging with others, be mindful how other people may be thinking and feeling. Really challenge yourself to walk in their shoes as best as possible. Simulating other people's difficulties often improves attitudes toward those people.

Acknowledge your bias and be honest with yourself about it. Pretending hurts progress. Be vulnerable and when appropriate, share with the other person what you are thinking and feeling and that you are actively challenging those biases. People appreciate vulnerability more than you know.

Focus on the other person. Minimize distractions when you are engaging with someone. It is hard to be empathetic when you are checking your phone or responding to the latest social media post. You can also focus by listening without comparing or contrasting. It is tempting to center the conversation around yourself, because after all, that's who you know the best, but keep the conversation focused on the other person.

Realize your limits. You can't be empathetic toward everyone all the time (I know some of those people and it's not healthy). It's important to start small. When engaged in conversation or research, give yourself time limits and realize when you need to temporarily step away to recharge, regroup, or simply refocus. You are needed for the long haul, not just the short-term.[15]

Avoid preferential empathy. This happens when you focus on showing empathy only to close friends and/or people who agree with you (people already in your circles). It is easier to be empathetic toward these people, as they are likely closer in our Circles of Grace. Challenge yourself to be more empathetic and hear the stories of those you do not understand or agree with (take the Six-Month Challenge).

Exercising empathy with others creates better unity and relationship capital, but it also prepares us for necessary tough conversations.

How to Have Difficult Conversations

It is never easy to have difficult conversations, but often they are necessary. Sometimes these conversations are either uncomfortable (because we don't want to address an issue), challenging (because it involves constructive or negative feedback), or both. You will find that many of the following suggestions are similar to the ones given earlier about dialogue and exercising empathy, and that is because these all flow together. No matter what type of difficult conversation you are entering, there are several things to consider.

Face your fear; don't flee it. Many people shy away from having tough or challenging conversations because they don't want to say the wrong thing, or they want to simply avoid the potential conflict. This may be a short-term solution, but it usually leads to long-term pain. Either address it immediately or, if you need to process, put it on your calendar so you won't back out. **Identify your own preconceptions.** What are you thinking and feeling about this person? Try to suspend those thoughts by writing them down. For example, I have a friend who rarely reaches out to me, and thus the narrative I have created is that I am just not that important to him anymore (self-centered perspective) versus being open to learning and understanding the changing dynamics for that person and their work.

Think positive. No, I am not talking about looking in the mirror and reciting twenty-one affirmations. Think positive about the person. Give them the benefit of the doubt and you will notice that how you communicate will also be more positive. Focus on the issue or problem at hand as well, and be careful not to attribute the difficulty to the person's identity (e.g., "No one with sense would ever say that").

Use "I feel/think" statements. It is important to focus on how you perceived what the person said. It is different when you say, "You were very rude and callous in yesterday's meeting" versus "I felt offended at some of the comments you made at yesterday's meeting." You should also put the emphasis on you versus assuming intent. Example: "Yesterday I felt offended when you cut me off in the meeting, and I don't think you meant to do that" versus "You offended me when you cut me off in the meeting. You don't value my perspective, do you?"

Avoid scope creep. Don't change the conversation or allow the conversation to be changed. Sometimes people change the conversation as a conditioned deflection technique. Politely ask if you can focus on the newly brought-up issue another time and ask to set up a time at the end of the conversation to address the issue that was brought up. Example: Person A: "I often feel like you talk over me." Person B: "Well, you are also constantly talking over me, and as a matter of fact, you are always on your phone or doing something else when I share." Person A: "I hear your concerns, but I would like to focus on my feelings of being talked over right now. Let's set up a time to address your concerns when we finish this conversation, okay? Can you understand why I feel talked over?"

Don't script it. You should definitely practice and have some "what if this happens" responses ready, but do not read from a script. For some people it can be helpful to have pointers or an outline, but do not read it word for word. You can write out what you want to say ahead of time, but it may be counterproductive to bring that script into the conversation with you. Sometimes things that appear too formal come off as disingenuous. Think about press conferences when someone apologizes for something they did wrong. If they read a statement word for word, they can come off as not really contrite, but when they engage with eye contact and speak from the heart (even if they went over what they would say ahead of time), it can feel more real to others.

Adopt a "no one has to lose" approach. Get away from the notion that someone has to win and someone has to lose, even if the other person does not share the same approach. Ask, "How would I feel tomorrow if . . ." Sometimes we do things in the heat of the moment. I certainly have done some things that at the moment felt good, but later on and especially the next day I asked myself why I did them. In that moment make an effort to remain calm and keep the focus on hearing and understanding, instead of trying to win the argument.

Avoid interrupting and absolutes at all costs. You will be tempted to interrupt, but practice makes perfect. Let the person finish; then wait two or three seconds before sharing your thoughts if you have anything to share. *Never* speak in absolutes. Use language that you would generally want to hear. If it would feel accusatory to you, then don't use it. Center the conversation on how you feel and how are experiencing the issue, not what you think the person's intent is.

Difficult conversations require intentionality, courage, and focus. It is important to be honest with people while not being overly harsh. Sometimes it's important to know when to agree to disagree or temporarily take a step back from the conversation.

Matt Aghedo and Civil Conversations

Matt Aghedo has been agreeing to disagree and sometimes taking a step back from conversations his whole life. Matt is the founder of Civil Conversations, and he birthed the organization partly because of his history with difficult conversations. When we talked in 2020, he said, "I used to hate difficult conversations. Now I enjoy them." He offered some practical tips on how to have civil conversations. He shared that relationships play a big role in civil conversations, because trusting that the other person has your best interests in mind is important.

However, whether you have a good relationship or not, he said, "Don't speak over each other, don't say intentionally inflammatory things, don't use extreme language like *always* and *never*, and do set the rules of engagement." He defines the rules of the engagement as identifying when the best time is to have the conversation and how to best have it. What do both parties agree will allow them to have a civil conversation? He said, "Both parties should communicate what it looks like for them to be heard." At the end of the day Matt understands that every conversation isn't going to go smoothly, but he offered this: "Giving people grace in conversations is huge, because sometimes people simply don't understand."[16] I would add that sometimes both parties don't understand or simply just don't agree.

How to Respectfully Disagree

Face it, we are going to disagree on things. Our experiences and education have shaped us into who we are today and what we value. I have noticed that people are not having a hard time disagreeing (that's pretty common). Where people are struggling is with *respectfully* disagreeing. Here are some tips that can help with that. You will notice some overlaps with the tips on having difficult conversations, and that is because respectfully disagreeing is part of a difficult conversation.

- Sometimes we don't have to reveal our disagreement. Some things aren't important enough. (You don't like the Baltimore Ravens? That's tough, but I probably won't tell you that I disagree with you and that you suck at life. Well, I might tell you I disagree with you, I just won't say you suck!)
- When disagreeing with someone, it is important to authentically acknowledge the other person's perspective. People don't expect everyone to agree all the time, but they do want to feel like you really heard them. We are so engulfed in a communication battle that very few people ever really feel heard.
- Don't disparage the person's belief (e.g., "I don't see how any sane person would believe in something like that").
- Don't make it personal. Stay focused on the topic, and don't take cheap shots. If you feel yourself going there, ask for a temporary break from the conversation.
- Try not to use "but," which can be seen as negating the statement that came before, even if it wasn't meant that way.
- Show the person respect. I often hear people say that unless you 100 percent agree with someone, you can't fully accept them, and this is simply not true. You can value that person as a person and still not agree with them 100 percent. This is an important part of society that we must regain. I have tons of friends who disagree with me politically, economically, religiously, and about matters of both financial and social concern, but they remain my friends.

- When disagreeing, don't speak in absolutes ("always" and "never"), as people very rarely always do one thing.
- See the person you disagree with as someone you love. How would you want someone to talk to your mother, or child, or your favorite aunt? Ask, "If I loved this person, how would I treat them?"
- Avoid interrupting at all costs. You will be tempted, but practice makes perfect. As I said earlier, let the person finish; then wait two or three seconds before sharing.
- See the issue from their perspective. Ask how their position could make sense to this person, even if you disagree.

At the end of the day, remember that you are dealing with a human being. One who is worthy of dignity, value, and respect no matter their beliefs or ideology. Let's get away from the notion that someone has to earn your respect, and let's start respecting people because of their humanity. When we better learn to respectfully disagree, it allows us to grow in our Inclusive Mindset because we see the value in others and their perspectives.

ACTION FORWARD

1. Have a dialogue with someone and practice suspending your thoughts and opinions in order not to advocate for side A or side B but rather create C.

2. Visit https://startempathy.org/ and identify one way you can show empathy to someone else.

3. Talk to a stranger who is different from you (e.g., if you don't have tattoos and would never get one, talk to someone who has one and hear their story).

Chapter 10

THE RIGHT-HAND PARADIGM™

How to Use Privilege
for the Good of Others

S everal years ago I was driving to an engagement and I stopped at
a country store. I forgot exactly what I was getting, but I remember being in the store and hearing this guy yell at the top of his lungs,
"These doors aren't made for left people!" My first reaction was to
wonder why this guy was yelling inside the store, and my second
reaction was one of confusion, because doors aren't made for right-
or left-handed people; they are just made for people, I thought.

His yelling intrigued me enough that I went to see what all
the fuss was about, and I noticed he was near one of those hot

dog–spinner machines. The left-side door opened up into a refrigerator, and it appeared the man had hit his hand and that was why he was yelling. Upon further inspection I noticed the right-side door opened into nothing, which led me to look further into left-handed people and their challenges.

THE PLIGHT OF LEFT-HANDED PEOPLE

As I started examining the research, I learned that left-handed people lived different lives than I did, and I had no idea. I learned that back in the day when students started school, they had to get to school early to claim the few left-handed desks (if there were any). I learned that some were taught it was a curse to be left-handed, and their parents forced them to write with their right hand. I learned that scissors that say they are multihanded are still made for . . . right-handed people. I learned from my left-handed business colleagues that they would get to dinner meetings early to claim the edge of the table so they weren't bumping into a right-handed person. I learned that doors, and cabinets, and a host of other things are made for right-handed people. I learned that left-handed surgeons aren't adequately equipped with left-handed tools during training.[1] I learned that most spiral notebooks are the bane of left-handed people's existence (since the spiral is on the left side).

I even solved one of the biggest mysteries at the National Institutes of Health (not really, but it sounds good). I was doing some work with their Equity, Diversity, and Inclusion team, and during the workshop they were able to solve a point of friction on the team. One of the members didn't like to share her pens, and people did not understand why. She shared in the session that she was left-handed, and that after an exhaustive search she had finally found some pens that didn't smear. She wasn't willing to give them up, especially because people tended not to return the pens after their use. By sharing the right-hand paradigm and inviting her to share her challenge as a left-handed person, we were able to address the reason behind the friction.

WHAT IS YOUR LUXURY?

I didn't know all of this information, nor did I know the challenges, because I didn't have to. I had no idea left-handed people lived this different life, because I had the "luxury" of not knowing. Doors were created for me, pens were created for me, spiral notebooks were created for me, and even multihanded scissors were created for me. Just because I had this luxury didn't make me a left-hand bigot (I am right-handed and proud), but it did give me certain advantages as a right-handed person in a society that has catered to my right-handedness. I also did nothing to earn being right-handed.

As I began diving deeper into those luxuries (not to be confused with better), I learned that I have luxuries in other areas as well, such as having two parents who graduated from college (one with a PhD in economics, and the other with a master's in psychology). I have the luxury of being a male in a society that has catered to men. I have the luxury of operating as a nondisabled person. I have so many luxuries. What about you? What are some of your luxuries?

This is not just about handedness; this is also about gender. This is not just about gender but also about sexuality. This is not just about sexuality but also about age. This is not just about age but also about race. This is not just about race but also about ability. This is not just about ability but about religion. This is not just about religion but about mental health. This is not just about mental health but about education. This is not just about education but about socioeconomics. This list could go on and on.

How has society catered to you? Having this luxury doesn't make you a bad person, but it should inspire you to help other people who don't have those same luxuries. With an Inclusive Mindset we look for ways to leverage our privilege for the good of the others. A few things I do for my lefties is that when I am leading an in-person training session and I have to assign seats, I look out for people who might be left-handed and I approach them and ask them if they would prefer to be on the edge. Sometimes I have to send out workbooks for my virtual attendees, and if they have to be bound, I place the spiral binding at the top rather than on the left side. If I had to give luxury a synonym, it would be privilege. One of the biggest challenges in this conversation is that often people in privileged groups do not realize they have privilege at all.

I have a family member who used to travel roughly two and a half hours for school to work on her advanced degree. She used Enterprise Rent-A-Car weekly so often that she got to know the manager, and the manager started giving her free upgrades. This happened for roughly two years until the manager moved on from that location. When my family member went to rent a car with the new manager she was given the car she paid for (without an upgrade), and she was livid. While she used to love Enterprise Rent-A-Car, now she thought of them as a bad company she would no longer rent from. She had this negative reaction because she got used to something that she did nothing to earn (free upgrades), and when that privilege was taken away, she felt she had been wronged. That is exactly how many of us feel when our privileges are challenged and addressed.

WHAT PRIVILEGE IS AND IS NOT

The term *privilege* can be linked to W. E. B. Dubois in the 1930s and Peggy McIntosh in the 1980s. Writer Sian Ferguson states, "We can define privilege as a set of unearned benefits given to people who fit into a specific social group. Society grants privilege to people because of certain aspects of their identity. Aspects of a person's identity can include race, class, gender, sexual orientation, language, geographical location, ability, and religion, to name a few."[2] One of the hardest parts of talking about privilege is all the misunderstandings about privilege. One has to also combat the notion that we have worked for everything we have (as if everyone has equal access to it), which, when you have certain privileges, is not entirely true. Maisha Z. Johnson wrote a powerful article on what privilege is and is not, where she identified eighteen aspects in a way that is much more precise and eloquent than I could ever create:

THE RIGHT-HAND PARADIGM | 117

1. Having privilege doesn't mean you're a bad person.
2. Having privilege means there's a whole system at work.
3. Having privilege doesn't mean you haven't experienced oppression in other ways.
4. Privilege can come in more than one form—and so can oppression.
5. Privilege isn't a contest to determine who's the most oppressed.
6. Having privilege means you can support the most vulnerable among us to strengthen your own fight.
7. Having privilege doesn't mean you didn't work hard or that you should feel bad about your good fortune.
8. Having privilege means a lot of people can't access what you have, no matter how hard they work.
9. Having privilege doesn't mean you've never been put down for that privileged identity.
10. Having privilege refers to systematic benefits for your identity (but the same identity trait may still attract incidents of prejudice).
11. Having privilege doesn't mean you're not a unique individual.
12. Having privilege means we all participate in discriminatory systems in different ways.
13. Pointing out privilege doesn't mean hating on the people who have it.
14. Pointing out privilege means supporting the privileged group to be fully human.
15. Having privilege doesn't mean your privilege is totally separate from the ways you're oppressed.
16. Having privilege means your benefits can be conditional.
17. Having privilege doesn't mean there's nothing you can do about it.
18. Having privilege means you have a choice about what to do with it.[3]

Do you see why I love this list? Which of the previous eighteen statements resonates with you the most? Number three really resonates with me because I used to think I didn't have privilege, but then I realized I faced classism. If you want to see a more detailed explanation of the items in that list, check out the article "What Privilege Really Means (and Doesn't Mean)—to Clear Up Your Doubts Once and for All."[4]

Melody Gross and Classism

Melody recalled a time when she was working for a non-profit and she had an encounter with her leader. Melody was a single mom who did not have a lot of money. One day Melody's son was really sick, and Melody shared she would need to stay home with him. Her leader (who was the same race and had also been a single mother) suggested she get a babysitter and come to work. While that seemed like a reasonable suggestion, Melody did not have the resources to afford a babysitter, and while she didn't think her leader had bad intentions, her leader did not understand her potential financial struggles. Her leader had high-powered jobs and was compensated well, so when things came up with her child, she could afford a babysitter. Melody was different. At the time she did not have the same support systems or finances her leader experienced.

In a 2020 interview I conducted with Melody, she offered this advice: "What are you doing in your personal life? Are you going to events with people that are different than you, and if you have children, where are you taking them in order for them to have different experiences? How can you recognize not everyone has the same privilege, and how can you use your privilege for the good of others?"[5]

Privilege and Power

Privilege is supported by power. That's why you won't see terms like *women privilege*, *nondisabled privilege*, *Black privilege*, or *poor privilege*. While there are certainly exceptions to this, the focus is on the rule. Usually those in a privileged category have people within the category who represent their identity in positions of power, even if the specific individual doesn't hold that same power. Sometimes those who are part of that privileged category have easier access to that power than those outside of that category. As an example, there are significantly more men in elected office and STEM (science, technology, engineering, and mathematics) industries, as we have been a patriarchal society. Therefore, if you are a man in one of these positions, it is important to wield your privilege for the good of women even when it doesn't feel personally good.

Oppression and Privilege

Oppression is the opposite of privilege, and those with privilege cannot be oppressed within their specific privileged group (e.g., while I may be oppressed as a Black person, I am not oppressed as a male). In simpler terms, just because I am privileged in one area of my life doesn't mean that I won't face oppression in another area. When certain things I may have gotten used to are either taken away or other people are given greater access to them, it may feel like oppression, but as Allan Johnson points out, "A group can be oppressed only if there exists another group with the power to oppress them."[6] When things we feel entitled to are addressed and potential wrongs are righted, it can really feel like we are losing something. An example of this could be as a non-disabled person like me having a plethora of parking spots open to them, and all of a sudden a large number of the parking spots closest to the front are designated for disabled people. I may feel a sense of loss, disappointment, and even frustration; but at the end of the day it is the right thing to do to have more designated parking spots for disabled people. That is the Inclusive Mindset. Allan Johnson states:

> The greatest barrier to change is that dominant groups, as we've discussed, don't see the trouble as their trouble, which means they don't feel obliged to do something about it. This happens for a variety of reasons—because they don't know the trouble exists in the first place, because they don't have to see the trouble as their trouble, because they're reluctant to give up privilege, because they feel angry and deprived and closed to the idea that they have privilege, because they're blinded by prejudice, because they're afraid of what will happen if they acknowledge the reality of privilege and oppression.[7]

HOW TO USE YOUR PRIVILEGE FOR GOOD

One of the first steps to using your status in a privileged group is to admit that privilege exists and that you have it. On many fronts this was hard for me initially and I was defensive, especially because I am in other marginalized groups, but as I started doing more research and having more conversations, it began to make sense and my heart began to shift. Having privilege is not necessarily a bad thing. It's all about what you do with it. When you are person who has privilege, if your only focus is your own advancement, or the advancement of people within your identity group, that is a misuse of your privilege. An example of this would be if I, as a male, focused only on advancing other males and did not notice or see the challenges that women face in the workplace and society.

While I don't always see everything, and never will, I recently noticed that a conference where I was speaking only had male speakers (and it wasn't a conference for men). I would not have been alert to that before, but as they started planning the conference for the next year, I was able to talk with the organizer and recommend they consider more women as speakers. While I know that won't solve all the unique challenges that women in our society face, it is at least something I can do to stand up for women.

Are you a bystander or an upstander? An upstander is a person who stands up to challenge injustices at both an individual level and a systemic level (e.g., challenging a person who is putting someone else down *and* helping change hiring policies within your organization). A bystander stands by when injustices occur (on any level) and does not commit to action. What will you commit to doing for others? Will you continue reading on issues of privilege, power, and oppression? Will you have conversations with people in groups that are not a part of a privileged category and learn their experiences? Will you commit to staying aware and opening your eyes and no longer avoiding or minimizing the effects of privilege? Will you take risks to stand up for and speak up for others? You are needed in this journey toward a more inclusive society.

ACTION FORWARD

1. Identify a left-handed person (if you are one, then someone else in a nonprivileged category) and ask about their experience and the unique challenges they have faced. How does that relate to other areas of "luxury"?

2. What is one "luxury" or privilege that you have, and what is a practical way you can use it for the good of those who don't have it? (For example: advocating for more accessible buildings for people with mobility challenges.)

3. When was the last time you saw someone experience injustice or mistreatment and you didn't do anything? Why not, and what will you do differently next time?

Chapter 11

THE MOVING WALKWAY

Advocacy, Allyship, and Being an Anti-

There were times when Otis Pickett feared for his life, his safety, and his job. Otis Pickett, a white Southerner with family Confederate ties, chose to join the fight against the Confederate imagery in the Mississippi state flag. Otis is clear that he is proud to be a Southerner and proud of his heritage, but an experience occurred that would forever change his perspective. Years ago, Otis attended a predominantly Black church that had a Black pastor. One of the things his pastor would do was visit all of the college students on campus. When it was Otis's turn, his pastor came to his fraternity house at his school in South Carolina. As his pastor was leaving, he noticed the pain in his pastor's face. His pastor obviously had seen the Confederate flags hanging in windows and on balconies. The hurt and pain transferred to Otis, as he never wanted to hurt his brother in Christ. Otis said, "Love for my 'neighbor' was more important than a symbol."

That experience and others inspired Otis to use his privilege for the good of others, and in 2016, he wrote an op-ed piece in the main newspaper in Jackson, Mississippi, where he was a history professor. In that op-ed he was careful to acknowledge those who had been doing the work before him and were presently doing the work of trying to get the Confederate emblem off of the Mississippi flag. After the paper was printed, he worried what the impact of his stand would be, but he said he would do it all over again. I spoke with Otis in 2020, and he shared, "If I lose my job or we are attacked, that means we are doing something, because we felt that what we were doing was right and showing love for people!" From his advocacy to remove Confederate imagery from the flag to his leadership in working to dismantle the school-to-prison pipeline, Otis took a stand. He said, "When people are in a posture of hurt, I like to move toward them and not from them."[1] This should be the sentiment we all share, even if it is against the moving crowd.

WHAT IS THE MOVING WALKWAY?

Have you been to the airport and seen one of those walkways that move? They're similar to escalators in the mall that take you from floor to floor, but they're flat. Dr. Beverly Tatum, author and president emerita of Spelman College, created the analogy of the moving walkway for how to deal with racism. Inspired by this analogy I have adapted it to talk about advocacy, allyship, and being an anti-. The moving walkway represents systems and policies in place that favor certain groups while oppressing other groups. While Dr. Tatum focused on racism, I am using it to talk about all different types of discrimination. I am bringing back the left-handed analogy from chapter 10, but you can easily substitute it for ageism, racism, sexism, ableism, heterosexism, classism, and other isms. I have found that there are four different types of people associated with the moving walkway: Blockers, Movers, Stoppers, and Disruptors.

1. **Blockers** (e.g., the handists): These are people who stand at the front of the moving walkway and try not to allow anyone who is not right-handed to get on the walkway. They feel that left-handed people are inferior to them, so they create and protect policies that disadvantage left-handed people.

2. **Movers** (e.g., the unconscious nonhandists): These are people who are not doing anything inherently against left-handed people. They aren't calling them names or standing in the way of their progress, but they also aren't doing anything to help left-handed people. They continue to walk on the moving walkways and wonder why everyone isn't taking advantage of the same opportunities afforded to them to continue moving ahead. They say to themselves, *I am glad I am not like those handists.*

3. **Stoppers** (e.g., the conscious nonhandists): Like Movers, these people aren't doing anything inherently against left-handed people. They have also noticed how bad the systems are, and they have decided to take a stand because it is unfair. They have decided to stop moving. They are not going to walk ahead like those Movers. They have stopped on the moving walkway. But even though they have stopped, the moving

walkway is still moving them ahead. While they may not be taking full advantage of the walkway, it is still moving them forward. They wonder how the Movers can live with themselves.

4. **Disruptors** (e.g., the anti-handists): These are people who notice the injustices and have chosen to go the opposite way on the moving walkway, disrupting the "natural" flow of things. People look at them strangely and wish they would turn around and go the "right" way. The other groups tell them they are going the wrong way, but that does not deter them. Going against the walkway is tiring, but it is worth it. They are going to get left-handed people and bring them on the walkway, and/or they are trying to figure out ways to dismantle the walkway all together.

Which one are you as it relates to sexism, ageism, racism, ableism, and other isms? This is not to make you feel guilt and shame, or to tell you that you are doing everything right. This is to encourage you that no matter where you are now, you can be an anti- on the moving walkway. We are either moving toward those who are marginalized and underrepresented or moving away from them. Some of the examples of walkway include established laws, institutional practices, and even cultural norms.[2]

In an article in *Harvard Business Review*, Robert Livingston uses a different metaphor to describe the moving walkway: fish in a stream. He states, "To help managers and employees understand how being embedded within a biased system can unwittingly influence outcomes and behaviors, I like to ask them to imagine being fish in a stream. In that stream, a current exerts force on everything in the water, moving it downstream."[3] Are you willing to swim upstream for others who are hurting or being left behind, or worse, oppressed by the water current?

ADVOCACY AND ALLYSHIP

There are a lot of semantics around advocacy and allyship, and there isn't one definition that everyone agrees upon (go figure). Some see advocacy as the highest form of standing up for others, while others see allyship as a higher form of advocacy. Some have even argued that activism is the highest form of support. What the words mean aren't as important to me as all of us stepping up for others in very important ways.

Advocacy and *allyship* aren't terms but ways of life. They are part of the Inclusive Mindset because they should become just who we are. While there may be confusion over the terms, there is not confusion that being an ally and an advocate requires consistent, sustained action over time.

I will focus the rest of this chapter on allyship and what it really means. Allyship isn't a badge of honor to be touted and shared with others, but rather a way of living. It is consistently acting on the behalf of others. Allyship is a shared investment. It's not about those people over there who are suffering, but rather all of us are suffering (even if you don't have the exact same experiences). It's not a "them"; it's a "we and us." You do not call yourself an ally, but based on your continued actions you are called an ally by others. If you are focused on being called an ally, then your focus is wrong, and it is self-centering versus focusing on others who are hurting.

Where to Start

Learn! Learn! Learn! I was recently inspired by good friend and generational diversity expert Raven Solomon, who shared with me the concept of beginner allyship.[4] It resonated with me so much that I decided to create a model to help people have a starting place if they want to know where to begin. I call it the 3x5 Beginner Allyship Model. This model does not now certify you as an ally, but it is a great start on a consistent journey of stepping up for others. In this model you commit to engaging three things in five areas: people, books, movies, podcasts/videos, and journal articles. If you have the luxury of having close friendships with people who are willing and emotionally available to offer you suggestions, that is awesome, but for four of the five areas you can utilize your favorite search engine of choice. Build relationships with people in different groups by asking friends to connect you, volunteering with organizations, and joining organizations that have a large contingency of this group. You can start with one of each five, or you can read all three books and then move to the next category. Remember, this is just the beginning of your journey, and if you consistently live out the actions of an ally, you will have done way more than fifteen as you advocate for others.

It is important to note that you may find the best information from those who are in the group you are engaging, rather than through an ally talking about that group. For example, if you are trying to learn more about those who are blind, it may be more beneficial to find three articles, three books, three movies, and three podcasts/videos authored by blind people. While there are always exceptions, as some allies have done a great job amplifying the stories of others, it can be helpful to hear and/or read directly from a person in that group.

This 3x5 Beginner Allyship Model is also designed to help you better understand the history (as well as the present issues) of the group you are choosing to engage. As you apply the model, it is important to listen, learn, act, and repeat (LLAR). Sometimes when I share this method, people say, "But doesn't listening require a person?" Sometimes it does, but you can also listen to what's going on in society. You can listen to all that is being shared (in videos and online), even if it is not a one-on-one meeting with an individual. Marginalized and underrepresented communities and identity groups have been talking, but sometimes we have been walking around with unintentional (and sometimes intentional) earplugs that keep us from hearing their voices (me included). When you operate by the Inclusive Mindset, you identify ways you can support others. Allyship becomes the norm for you.

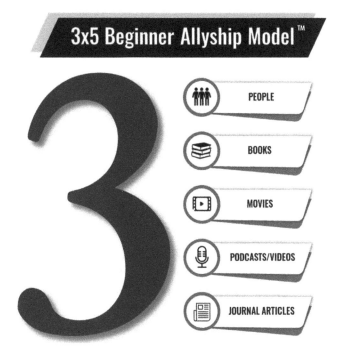

3x5 Beginner Allyship Model™

- PEOPLE
- BOOKS
- MOVIES
- PODCASTS/VIDEOS
- JOURNAL ARTICLES

Raven Solomon and Authentic Allyship

Raven is an expert on generational diversity, and her passion for allyship is evident. She shared a few ways we can be better allies. When I interviewed Raven, she said one of the first steps is "look to the place you currently have influence." Sometimes people think they have to change the world when they should first focus on influencing the world right around them. Raven challenges others to "not to get caught up into the title! Don't look at *ally* as a noun but look at it as a verb." She also said, "Allyship is both active and consistent." No matter where we are, what position we hold, or what our background is, we can be an ally for others.[5]

Ten Tips for Allyship

Here are a few tips that can help us along the journey toward becoming active and consistent allies:

1. Take on the mantra of airport security: "If you see something, say something." Don't stand by if you see discrimination happening. I hope we wouldn't stand by if we saw one of our children or nieces or nephews being bullied. Discrimination is an unstated form of bullying. Learn and practice the skills of challenging oppressive remarks, behaviors, policies, and institutional structures.

2. Take ownership of educating yourself about others' oppression, even if you can't fully understand exactly what it feels like. For example, I currently do not know what it is like to be deaf, but that shouldn't stop me from taking on their issues as my own.

3. Engage and join organizations online and in person.

4. Reflect and consider your own biases and privileges toward that issue or group. Examine and challenge your prejudices, stereotypes, and assumptions.

5. Work through feelings of guilt, shame, and defensiveness to understand what is beneath them and what needs to be healed (sometimes with a counselor).

6. Expect to make mistakes. It is a part of the journey and that is okay. If you waited for perfect, you would wait for a long time. You should also seek feedback on ways you can learn from those mistakes.

7. Learn about those who have been and are currently doing the work and find ways to honor and amplify their voices.

8. Give of your time and resources to organizations that are specifically addressing this issue. Become a member, subscribe to their newsletter, and learn more about what is going on.

9. Do your own research and don't expect to be taught (by marginalized individuals) how to be an ally, but if someone is willing to help you, be appreciative.
10. Act collaboratively with members of the marginalized group to dismantle oppression.

Don't pursue allyship to be called an ally; pursue it because it is the right thing to do. Allyship should and will cost you something; if nothing else it will cost you comfort, because you are going the "wrong" way on the walkway, and people dislike when you disrupt the normal flow of things, but that is what an anti- does.

BEING AN ANTI-

Remember the Disruptors (anti-handists) from the moving walkway analogy earlier? When you are an anti-racist, anti-ageist, anti-sexist, anti-ableist, and so on, it is important that you accept the role you have played in harming a marginalized community, whether through your direct actions or inaction (e.g., I have contributed to gender inequities by ignoring and even at times justifying pay gaps. I was so focused on showing the nuances of why there is a pay gap that I did not really take the time to listen, learn, and process the challenges that women face in the workplace). To be an anti- means you acknowledge that you are not better than the group you are advocating for. You are not some special gift sent down to help these poor destitute people. You acknowledge that you are not superior. On the other hand, you do not have to do what I see some people doing as they support marginalized groups. They put themselves down and communicate their own perceived inferiority. *In order to be an anti-, you acknowledge you are neither superior nor inferior. You are simply different and ready to serve.*

When you are an anti- you hold yourself and others accountable. You don't have to fully understand their experiences and journeys, but you do have to be fully present with them as they share them. This presence leads to having meaningful conversations with people about their experiences (and being okay if they are unable to discuss them with you right now). Not only will going to a presentation or workshop or training help to educate you, but over time you might consider leading them yourself or creating a space for someone in that marginalized group to do it. Let's talk about anti-racism as a specific example of this.

There are certain issues that rise to the top of our social consciousness throughout history, and one that is prevalent today is racial inequity and injustice. What has risen to combat that is anti-racism education and anti-racist allies. In discussing ways to be anti-racist, Robert Livingston states, "Racism has less to do with what's in your heart or mind and more to do with how your actions or inactions amplify or enable system dynamics already in place."[6]

Some people believe that not being a racist is the opposite of being a racist, and this is not the case, because it signifies neutrality, which isn't safe for those being oppressed. Anti-racism is the opposite because it actively confronts both the individuals and the systems that support it. Ibram X. Kendi, the author of *How to Be an Antiracist*, states, "The good news is that racist and antiracist are not fixed identities. We can be a racist one minute and an anti-racist the next. What we say about race, what we do about race, in each moment, determines what—not who—we are."[7] While race is a powerful example, how will you learn to stand up for others who are feeling injustices regardless of race? This is in total agreement with the Inclusive Mindset, because the skill sets to consistently operate by the Inclusive Mindset can be learned. You and I can continue growing and learning, but it will require us to take meaningful action. We must do something!

ACTION FORWARD

1. Visit a museum dedicated to the history of an under-represented or marginalized group, such as an African American museum or a Native American museum.

2. Pick an identity group that is not your own. Which of the four types of people best fits you on the moving walkway toward this group? Why do you think that is? How can you be more consistently a Disruptor (anti-)?

3. What is one tip for allyship that you can commit to doing?

Chapter 12

THE GLASS HALF ...

Activating Your Attitude
and Actions

M any years ago a "motivational" speaker came to my organization. He held up a glass on stage and asked the audience
if the glass was half empty or half full. I knew the right answer
was half full, but I wasn't feeling particularly motivated at the time,
so I remained silent. I remembered being twenty-five and going
through one of the toughest times of my life. Quarter-life crisis,
guess it happens. I was lying in bed, looking at this glass on the
nightstand that was half whatever of some clear liquid (it may have

been water, it may not have been . . . I was twenty-five) and saying to myself, *Just see the glass half full.* I started reciting, "Half full, half full, half full," trying to will myself to believe it. All of a sudden I stopped and asked myself, *Why am I asking if the glass is half empty or half full when I can just fill the glass back up?*

Filling the glass up takes action. It's easy to talk about the glass and pontificate (SAT word) on its current state, but it's much harder to get a pitcher and fill that glass back up. This is the beauty of the Inclusive Mindset—we can fill the glass back up with progress, growth, and development. We have the opportunity to embrace the opportunity to consistently get 1 percent better each day, and that is exciting. What will you do to continue this journey and fill up not only your glass but those around you?

HOW TO FILL YOUR GLASS EVERY DAY

Who is the only person you and I can control? You guessed it: the person who disagrees with you. Just kidding! We can only control ourselves, and we have to remind ourselves of that each and every day. In my "Work to a Different Beat" presentation, one of my favorite sayings is "It's not about finding meaning in your work; it's about bringing meaning to your work!" The former is focused on all the things happening outside of yourself, and the latter is focusing on what you choose to do and believe. You are the only person in charge and control of your growth, so what will you do to grow? I love that we are not stuck in our ways. I love that we can teach a slightly older dog (and cat, for inclusivity purposes) new tricks.

Research confirms that our brains rewire when we are learning, especially deep learning.[1] One way to continue your quest for learning and not be discouraged where you currently are is "I am not yet" statements. "*I* am not learning about gender equity . . . *yet*; *I* am not speaking up for people with impaired sight . . . *yet*; *I* am not identifying ways to create a better hiring process for socioeconomically disadvantaged applicants . . . *yet.*" The power of the "yet" is that it provides hope and a sense of future. What is one area you want to grow in that you haven't grown in . . . yet? This is the best attitude to have as we continue cultivating an Inclusive Mindset.

Another way to fill your cup every day is with intentionality. One of the unique challenges in our culture today is that there is an overemphasis on things happening organically. Organic action isn't going to get us out of the mess of injustice and oppression that we are in. It's also not going to help you and me operate in the Inclusive Mindset. We need to be intentional, and over time what we do will become natural and simply flow out of us.

Do you remember learning how to ride a bike? I don't, but I do remember teaching my daughter how to ride. I remember putting on the training wheels and seeing her ride through the streets of the community. I remember her stumbling quite a bit and falling. I remember when she started getting better and we were able to take off the training wheels. I remember the confidence she began to build as she kept practicing, even through her falls. Now my princess can ride with one hand and turn very fast, and it is quite natural for her. She kept learning, and we followed the plan to help her be able to ride. Acting on behalf of others is a similarly learned behavior.

Accountability is also of great help in developing the Inclusive Mindset. Go on this journey with someone else. I love the African proverb that says, "If you want to go fast, go alone. If you want to go far, go together." Learn together and find ways you can support each other as you listen, learn, act, and repeat. Accountability will challenge you to keep going even when things get tough. Even when you make a mess of things. Even when you don't know what to do, this can help you stay focused and give it the attention it deserves. Psychologist and author Rick Hanson states, "In particular, because of what's called 'experience-dependent neuroplasticity,' whatever you hold in attention has a special power to change your brain. Attention is like a combination spotlight and vacuum cleaner: it illuminates what it rests upon and then sucks it into your brain—and your self."[2]

138 THE INCLUSIVE MINDSET

Lastly, while it is important to have a sense of urgency because real people are hurting and real lives need advocacy and allyship, remember you are a finite being. You can't do everything, and you will likely burn out if you take that approach. I've seen this time and time again with teachers who are committed to supporting marginalized communities. They have a good three-to-five-year run and then they burn out. I am not saying move slowly, because you may be able to go harder than you have been going, but I am saying you are needed for the long haul. Do you remember "The Tortoise and the Hare" story? The hare got off to an impressive start and dazzled everyone with his speed, while the tortoise was slow and steady getting to the finish line.

Be the tortoise. What I notice is that whenever major events happen in our society, a lot of "hares" come out and look really good for a little bit; then they are nowhere to be found (that's also been me). A lot of people have become hares and show flashes of movement, but the tortoise persists over time. Make small changes in a big way that can lead to sustained growth by developing inclusivity as a habit.

HABIT FORMATION

What stops you from acting on what you know to be true? What stops you from being more inclusive, from enlarging your circles with those who are different, from hearing perspectives you disagree with, from standing up for others who are being marginalized? It's a four-letter word. *Fear.* We are afraid of what people will say; we are afraid to fail and make mistakes; we are afraid of the impact it will have on our careers and families. We have to lean into that fear and do what is right. I love what fear expert and my good buddy Darryl Bellamy says about overcoming fear: "Fearlessness is waking up every day and asking yourself, 'What small step can I take today?'" That's it. The Inclusive Mindset is focused on how you can take small steps every day to grow. When you get a chance, you will look back and see how far you've come.

You will see the habits forming in you of curiosity, deep listening, and wonderment.

Habits are important because the research shows that when something reaches the habit level, it continues even when motivation or interest has decreased. It just becomes something you do. When we do things over and over again it becomes natural. When is the last time you thought about how to tie your shoes (unless you saw that TED Talk on tying your shoes wrong)? Small but specific actions are most likely to lead to habit formation. Every day we should strive to learn one thing about someone, or a topic area related to diversity and inclusion. It can be five minutes or five hours, but build the habit to keep learning.

Consider journaling your thoughts and what you might have learned over the course of that day about yourself and about others. Consider doing something like this for two or three months. As we talked about in chapter 2, it's been found that on average it takes sixty-six days to form a habit (sometimes shorter and sometimes longer).[3] When something is a habit, it feels strange not to do it. I want it to feel strange for us when we aren't curious, authentically listening, and stepping up for others. But it will first require a plan.

THE INCLUSIVE MINDSET PLAN (IMP)™

Over the last decade I've worked with everyone from Fortune 50 leaders to fourth graders on this concept of the Inclusive Mindset, and one thing I've found that has been consistent is that people like having a direction on where to start. Sometimes it can feel so overwhelming and you may not know where to begin. You may choose to put together an Inclusive Mindset Plan (IMP) to help you on your journey. To be clear, this plan will not solve the ills of our society and it is not exhaustive, but it will help you get started and keep going.

For my nonplanners who just like to wing it, let me provide a little research for you. A study was conducted on exercise using three groups. Group 1 was asked to track how often they exercised.

Group 2 was asked to track their exercises and read materials on why exercise is beneficial. Researchers also informed Group 2 how exercise could help them. Group 3 received everything that Group 2 did, and they were told to create a plan for when and where they would exercise. The first two groups reported 35 to 38 percent of people exercising at least once per week, while 91 percent of the third group exercised at least once per week. They call this phenomenon "implementation intentions."[4] Having a plan can help you start and keep going. (For a more in-depth Inclusive Mindset template, visit theinclusivemindset.com.)

What I am about to share is not an all-encompassing plan, but it is a way forward. You can play around with the frequencies, but the key point is that you are taking meaningful action consistently. Things to consider in your plan are what you will do daily, weekly, monthly, quarterly, and yearly. You will want to place this on your calendar and give it a time and space, because based on research I included in my last book, *Your Why Matters Now*, you are more likely to do it when it moves from your to-do list to your calendar. Here are some suggestion for your IMP:

Daily:

- At the end of the day, ask what you learned about something or someone who is different from you in an area where you want to grow. If you didn't learn anything, what will you intentionally learn tomorrow?
- Ask yourself if you were inclusive today and where you could have been a little more inclusive of others.

Weekly:

- Have a conversation with a stranger (trash collector, neighbor, Amazon delivery person. You know you see them almost every day at your place of residence).
- Get on a video-conference call with someone. Ask to be introduced to people from a different identity group

(e.g., if you are from an urban city ask to be connected to someone from a rural city).

- Listen to a podcast or watch a video on an area of interest.

Monthly:

- Visit a museum or an exhibit of a different and/or marginalized group in person or virtually.
- Intentionally uplift or amplify a voice of someone from a marginalized community.

Quarterly:

- Volunteer with an organization that is working to deal with discrimination or helping an identity group you have chosen to focus on.
- Utilize the 3x5 Beginner Allyship Model to continue learning and growing.

Yearly:

- Do two Six-Month Challenges, one in an area you are unfamiliar with, and one in an area you disagree with (see chapter 5).
- Donate to an organization serving a marginalized group.

So, what will you do? What is one thing you will commit to?

WHAT'S NEXT?

As I shared earlier, this is not the be-all and end-all. For some of you this will be a continuation of a journey you are already on, and for others this is the beginning of your journey. The fact of the matter is that this is a journey. The Inclusive Mindset isn't something to be achieved but rather something to be lived that requires continued growth. We have the opportunity to create a world where people are treated with value, dignity, and respect no matter what they look like, how they identify, or what they believe. Where people engage others every day with a sense of wonderment and curiosity. Where people disagree respectfully while honoring the perspective of others. Where everyone feels included, seen, and heard; and the voices of the marginalized are elevated and amplified. Where people stand up for others when they see injustice occurring and challenge systems that don't work for others. Where people don't have to be perfect and can receive grace as they learn from their mistakes. Where diversity and inclusion are no longer an initiative but are a part of our everyday lives. Where it is no longer a mandate but simply a mindset.

What will you do with your opportunity to create this world? I hope you will choose to keep growing, learning, and moving forward, because the human beings who are in the world and are yet to be born deserve it.

There are a couple more things to consider as you continue growing in the Inclusive Mindset. Why don't you tell three to five people what you learned and the one thing you have committed to doing over the next two or three months? This increases your likelihood of actually doing it. Also, as I said earlier, this journey is best done with others, so consider walking with someone and ask for accountability where you all meet once a month to discuss what you are learning and how you are growing. Some organizations have done this in a book-club format.

No matter what you do, please never stop growing, learning, and developing. You are vital for the vision of a more inclusive world.

ACTION FORWARD

1. Identify a person who would be willing to take the journey with you toward a more Inclusive Mindset.

Talk to them and pick a starting date for your monthly meetings.

2. Start your Inclusive Mindset Plan and identify one thing you can do daily to become more inclusive.

3. Choose an area that you want to dive deeper into and write down the following:

   ▶ What is your current experience with this topic?

   ▶ What are your current assumptions and attitudes toward this topic?

   ▶ What questions do you have about this specific topic?

   Start researching the answers on your own. If you get stuck, connect with someone you trust who is emotionally available to help you find the answer.

HOW TO BE
AN INTENTIONALLY
INCLUSIVE LEADER

Elizabeth McKee, the executive director of Leadership Charlotte, was faced with a choice. Should she encourage Sarah to apply for the upcoming Leadership Charlotte cohort? Elizabeth had been approached by an organization that a fellow Leadership Charlotte alumnus worked for, and they had asked her to consider a high-functioning woman with Down syndrome to be in the cohort. Elizabeth decided to encourage Sarah to apply. Elizabeth shared that she made the decision "despite some potential challenges from others in the cohort." A lot of people in the class ended up really supporting Sarah, and the group learned a lot from her and her experience. When I spoke with Elizabeth in 2020, she shared, "I didn't wave a magic wand and grant her access. . . . I simply encouraged her to interview. She went through the same process as everyone."[1]

Elizabeth says, as an inclusive leader, "you have to be willing to not be liked." When you step up for others, sometimes you will get backlash, but you have to see it as worth it. Elizabeth and the people who suggested Sarah are great examples of Intentionally Inclusive Leaders who, despite some initial pushback, did what was right, and the cohort participants were better for it.

WHAT IS AN INTENTIONALLY INCLUSIVE LEADER (IIL)™?

"Corporate leaders may not be able to change the world, but they can certainly change their world."[2] Being an Intentionally Inclusive Leader does not happen by chance. It takes focus, dedication, and great humility. It is not an easy lift, as it is easier to simply focus on oneself. I have found that *everyone wants to be a leader until they realize what it takes to actually lead others.* Intentionally Inclusive Leaders first apply the principles of the Inclusive Mindset to themselves, and then they map a path forward for others. In an article for *Harvard Business Review*, Robin Ely and David Thomas state,

> Leaders are the stewards of an organization's culture; their behaviors and mindsets reverberate throughout the organization. Hence to dismantle systems of discrimination and subordination, leaders must undergo the same shifts of heart, mind, and behavior that they want for the organization as a whole and then translate those personal shifts into real, lasting change in their companies."[3]

I believe long-lasting change starts with the personal, and the personal then impacts people professionally. Leadership starts with you before it can impact anyone else, and that is why I share with leaders and CEOs that their first step should not always be in their organizations but in their personal lives. I am not saying to hold off the process of inclusivity within your teams and organizations; however, often the longevity of such efforts hinges upon the genuine commitment to it. If you aren't willing to commit personally, why will it last professionally? Not only do leaders focus on their internal development, but they also bring others along with them in ways beyond just being told to do so.

Intentionally Inclusive Leaders cultivate an environment that increases and encourages inclusivity. They also, as Michael Slepian states, "create environments where employees feel comfortable speaking up when they see something that does not seem inclusive."[4] They create a place where others feel they are valued and can belong. *Harvard Business Review* reported:

> When employees felt included, involved, and accepted (real inclusion), they felt like they belonged in the workplace. When employees felt like others asked for their input only because they were supposed to, or sought their opinion as someone who can represent their social group (surface inclusion), they felt like they belonged *less*. When being included for surface-level reasons, such as seeking a minority opinion, people can feel singled out on the basis of their demographics. This reduced sense of belonging works directly against inclusion efforts.[5]

In reviewing the literature, one thing I consistently see is the impact IILs have on recruiting efforts within their organizations. IILs don't just recruit people who are underrepresented, but they also retain and develop their talent. IILs leverage underrepresented individuals' experiences and knowledge by creating an environment where different points of view are valued and not minimized. *It's not just about having more diversity, but rather about cultivating and leveraging that diversity to learn, grow, and progress.*

Ely and Thomas shared four actions to help leaders shift to a more meaningful approach with diversity and inclusion:

1. Build trust: develop a workplace where people feel open to express themselves freely.
2. Actively work against discrimination and subordination: be willing to combat discrimination and communication by words and actions that it won't be tolerated.
3. Embrace a wide range of styles and voices: challenge organizational norms that may favor a dominant group (e.g., workplace hair and dress codes).
4. Make cultural differences a resource for learning: create opportunities for discussion about experiences in and out of the workplace.[6]

The first action—build trust—is foundational, because without trust, employees and team members will see efforts as tokenism, mere words, or worse. Trust as a foundation is echoed by Korn Ferry research, which states that the five disciplines of an inclusive leader are that he or she (1) builds interpersonal trust, (2) integrates diverse perspectives, (3) optimizes talent, (4) applies an adaptive mindset, and (5) achieves transformation.[7] When people trust the leader and/or organization, they are more likely to feel safe showing up to work as their true selves, as well as speaking up for themselves and for others. Juliet Bourke of Deloitte Australia stated, "Inclusive leaders understand that people are most collaborative when they feel safe to contribute without fear of embarrassment or punishment. They understand that power dynamics, dominating styles, and low tolerance of differences can stop team members from speaking up."[8]

FROM THE BUSINESS CASE
TO THE HUMANITY CASE

There has been much talk of the business case of diversity (I discussed it in chapter 3). A business case can be defined as justification for a proposed project based on projected commercial benefits. Since the term first emerged in the late 1980s, it has been used to highlight the benefits of a highly diverse organization. These benefits include higher profit, better decision-making, and an overall competitive advantage. This outcome is confirmed by McKinsey & Company, whose research shows that the most diverse companies are "more likely to outperform their [less diverse] peers on profitability" (with a focus on gender, ethnic, and cultural diversity).[9] However, just having diversity does not lead to higher profits, because it is all about what you do with it.

The business case has been proven to be advantageous in several ways. A McKinsey & Company report, *Delivering Through Diversity*, states: "*Why Diversity Matters* research established a statistically significant correlation—without claiming a causal relationship—between greater levels of diversity in company leadership and a greater likelihood of outperforming the relevant industry peer group on a key financial performance measure, profitability."[10] The business case is important, but it is not enough. Robin Ely and David Thomas echo that sentiment when they say, "Scholarly researchers have rarely found that increased diversity leads to improved financial outcomes. They *have* found that it leads to higher-quality work, better decision-making, greater team satisfaction, and more equality—under certain circumstances."[11] They go on to state,

> Business leaders and diversity advocates alike are advancing a simplistic and empirically unsubstantiated version of the business case. They misconstrue or ignore what abundant research has now made clear: Increasing the numbers of traditionally underrepresented people in your workforce does not *automatically* produce benefits. Taking an "add diversity and stir" approach, while business continues as usual, will not spur leaps in your firm's effectiveness or financial performance.[12]

The business case shouldn't be the primary focus. Instead, why not focus on the humanity case for including those who are different and eradicating discrimination from our workplaces? The humanity case is simply valuing and promoting diversity and inclusion because it is the right thing to do. In a *Fast Company* article, Sarah Kaplan shares, "Corporate leaders would be better served if they stopped trying to justify diversity with profit margins and stock charts—a mentality that can ultimately hurt the very groups these policies are meant to help—and instead embrace diversity because it is the right thing to do."[13] The humanity case focuses on recruiting, retaining, leveraging, and amplifying marginalized and underrepresented groups not because it is more profitable, but because organizational leaders value these groups and how they make their organizations better.

Just increasing marginalized or underrepresented groups doesn't add value if they do not feel respected. Simply being brought in to increase diversity numbers or help the organization fulfill quotas or an empty diversity and inclusion statement misses the mark of true diversity and inclusion and of addressing existing inequities. Employees don't feel valued and respected if they feel organizations have to justify hiring them and leveraging their talents with financial projections. Ely and Thomas cement their perspective when they write, "We are disturbed by the implication that there must be economic grounds to justify investing in people from underrepresented groups. Why should anyone need an economic rationale for affirming the agency and dignity of any group of human beings? We should make the necessary investment because doing so honors our own and others' humanity and gives our lives meaning."[14]

I advocate a shift away from the business case and toward the humanity case, where we create spaces for all types of people to engage and be part of the fabric of amazing organizations. Ely and Thomas continue, "Being genuinely valued and respected involves more than just feeling included. It involves having the power to help set the agenda, influence what—and how—work is done, have one's needs and interests taken into account, and have one's contributions recognized and rewarded with further opportunities to contribute and advance."[15] This is not to say that promoting and valuing diversity and inclusion won't come with its share of challenges, as all change does. That is why it is paramount for organizational leaders to see the importance of diversity beyond dollars and cents. Kaplan states, "Only the organizations that invest heavily in building their inclusion muscles are going to reap the benefits of diversity. What this says is that gaining the benefits of diversity also requires serious investments in organizational transformation."[16]

A Gym and Intentional Inclusion

In Barcelona, Spain, the gym Sant Pau is run by leaders who are intentional about inclusion and about serving the needs of the underrepresented. After an initial 2012 bankruptcy, the employees bought the gym in an effort to better serve their community. In a broadcast interview on BBC Reel, the gym's cooperative manager, Ernest Morera, shared, "This is a special place. This is a company that was taken up by its employees, with eighty years of history. Once we took it over, we thought we had a responsibility towards our surroundings."[17] This demonstrates one of the true signs of great leaders: they aren't told what to do, but rather they sense responsibility to do the right thing. And boy are they doing some right things.

Sant Pau has five hundred paid members, as well as more than nine hundred patrons who do not pay anything because they cannot afford to. The pool is closed on Fridays for Muslim women, they offer changing rooms and swim classes for trans people (which has become its most popular swim class), and they currently average 3,500 showers a month for the homeless. Additionally, several of its current workers were homeless at the time they were hired. These workers say the gym is where they have developed a sense of belonging and where they are valued as members of the community.

It is evident why this gym is much different from many others you might encounter. While the space and its leadership are far from perfect, the workers' simple desire to help the vulnerable, to listen to their neighbors, and to find helpful ways to serve others provides a clear example for leaders who want to be intentionally inclusive. As a leader, what sense of responsibility have you begun to notice as you serve those you lead, and what will you change in yourself, your organization, your team, and your community?

CHANGE MANAGEMENT

Change is hard! That's why having a clear and defined "why" is foundational. While there are many change processes, I have found ADKAR (also the title of a book by Jeff Hiatt) to be the most beneficial.[18] The ADKAR process is one that I've used, implemented, and observed in both small and large companies. The process is much more in-depth than what I will cover here, but the summary is still valuable to leaders who want to make meaningful change in diversity and inclusion. The ADKAR process states that five things have to happen for long-lasting change to occur: (1) *Awareness* of the need for change, (2) *desire* to support the change, (3) *knowledge* of how to change, (4) *ability* to demonstrate skills and behaviors, and (5) *reinforcement* to make the change stick.[19] As you think through cultivating the Inclusive Mindset in your organization and team, consider these five steps as a way to craft a long-standing culture of diversity and inclusion. True change starts with leadership committing to a course of action. True change starts with the leader modeling the behavior they want to see within their team and/or organization. What one change will you commit to modeling?

Change is often uncomfortable and challenging, but the right changes are rewarding. In addressing how people can be better inclusive leaders, Jennifer Brown shares, "Leaders should be uncomfortable if they're leading in the right way."[20] Don't wait until it feels right, but start because it is right. Charlotte Sweeney and Fleur Bothwick share in *Inclusive Leadership* that "creating change, getting people to think differently and do things in ways that they may have never done in the past, will not come without its challenges."[21] If you are not receiving resistance to your diversity and inclusion efforts, then you may not be making the right kind of changes, or you may not be going far enough.

Kim Davis and Putting People First

Kim Davis, the chief diversity and inclusion officer for the insurance company NFP, takes it a step further and says that in order to have lasting change, you have to start with asking how you are putting your people first . . . period! In order to do that, she says, it is important to partner strategy with people. Without a strategy to carry any change effort forward, especially increasing diversity and inclusion within organizations, the change will be short lived. I spoke with Kim in 2020, and she said, "Focusing on one issue without a foundation to carry it forward won't work!"[22]

FIFTEEN TIPS FOR AN INTENTIONALLY INCLUSIVE LEADER

While this list is certainly not exhaustive, it is helpful to identify two or three things you can commit to in order to create an Inclusive Mindset Organization (IMO) or team. All the tips require committed, sustained action to be helpful.

1. Be humble. The bedrock of Inclusive Leadership is to realize that it is not about you. In *The Six Signature Traits of Inclusive Leadership*, Bernadette Dillon and Juliet Bourke state, "Inclusive leaders have the courage to speak out about themselves and to reveal, in a very personal way, their own limitations. Instead of shying away from the challenge of imperfection, highly inclusive leaders adopt an attitude of humility. In 2014, the US-based think tank Catalyst identified 'humility' as one of the four leadership behaviors that predicated whether employees felt included."[23]

2. Express empathy. Feeling the pain of your people and seeing things from their perspective is vital to leading others. In the article "Empathy Stats and Facts for Business," Brand Genetics states,

> In studies by the Management Research Group, empathy was found to be the top competence for good leadership and one of the three strongest predictors of senior executive effectiveness. Similar results were found by 2016 CCL analysis of 6,731 leaders from 38 countries, where enhanced empathy was linked to superior performance. A recent DDI analysis of high performing leadership with 15,000 business leaders confirmed the same link between empathy and leadership performance. More worrying was the finding that empathy remains low in business leaders, with only 40% having proficient empathy skills.[24]

3. Build trust. Leaders address unfairness, mistreatment, or discrimination, even if doing so creates consequences for their business. One of my clients recently shared with me an instance when she heard a client say some disparaging remarks that impacted a few of her team members in one of their business meetings. She was a little fearful to address it, but she leaned into that fear and brought it up with her client. Her team was grateful and felt she had their best interests in mind, even though there was the potential for limited negative business consequences. She earned the trust of her team by standing up for them in the face of potential business loss.

4. Lead with vulnerability. Intentionally Inclusive Leaders should, like Ely and Thomas say, "reach out from a place of vulnerability, as a way of creating connection and psychological safety, rather than staying silent from a place of privilege and self-protection."[25] It is important for leaders to acknowledge their blind spots and to be open with their team about how they are addressing them. People aren't expecting perfect leaders but rather real ones.

5. See your people. In being an Intentionally Inclusive Leader, it is paramount to embrace your direct reports or those you serve as individuals, as well as being part of their collective identity groups. They do not represent their group differences (e.g., they do not represent all blind people, all people from the South, or all South Asians). Instead, learn from them. Practical methods of doing so are to conduct focus groups with underrepresented or marginalized employees and/or one-on-one meetings to best understand their unique perspectives, feedback, and issues. Ask questions like "What would help you to be fully seen at work?" "What can I do to help you to bring your full self to work every day?" "Is there anything hindering you from bringing your full and best self to work?"

6. Seek feedback. It is imperative that Inclusive Leaders see complaints and/or feedback about ways they and the company can build diversity and inclusion not as threats but as opportunities for progress and growth. Employees are less likely to share their honest thoughts if they feel that retaliation may occur. It's not good enough to just take criticism; you need to invite it. While leaders can't do or fix everything, they can share progress and honest perspectives on steps forward.

7. Focus on progress. Intentionally Inclusive Leaders are okay with not getting it perfect or just right, because that criteria can stop them from having discussions and creating dialogue that will help move the conversation forward in meaningful ways. In a Q&A with *HR Magazine* about how to have positive change, Ben Hasan (senior vice president and chief culture, diversity, and inclusion officer at Walmart) says, "We don't have all the answers, but we know we can't afford to wait to figure everything out."[26]

8. Facilitate dialogue. Inclusive Leaders create spaces for dialogue where people can understand others' experiences. One of the most effective ways to develop a culture of empathy is opening up spaces for people to honestly share and listen.[27] Daniel Fajardo, a diversity committee member of a Toyota Financial Services customer service center, shared with me that they not only created a Lunch and Learn series, but they also created informal opportunities for people to share their stories and experiences with others.[28]

9. Be accountable. We measure what we value. Robert Livingston states, "Organizations can integrate diversity and inclusion into managers' scorecards for raises and promotions—if they think it's important enough."[29] In another *Harvard Business Review* article, David Pedulla shares why it's important to be accountable:

> Set goals, collect data, and examine change over time and in comparison to other organizations: When it comes to maximizing profits and effectiveness, many businesses deploy this set of strategies. Why not do the same for issues of diversity and inclusion? Sociologists Elizabeth Hirsh at University of British Columbia and Donald Tomaskovic-Devey at University of Massachusetts at Amherst argue that companies should do precisely this.[30]

Have a clear strategy for how you will really move the needle in diversity and inclusion efforts.

10. Praise progress and effort. Praise people for their meaningful efforts around diversity and inclusion, not just for achieving the right outcome. Carol Dweck discusses a study in which the researchers praised two different groups of students. One group was praised for their ability ("Wow, you got . . . eight right. . . . You must be smart at this"), and the other group was praised for their effort ("Wow, you got . . . eight right. . . . You must have worked really hard"). In the beginning both groups were equal, but the results began to change after they were praised. Talking about the ability praise group, Dweck states, "When we gave them a choice, they rejected a challenging new task that they could learn from. They didn't want to do anything that could expose their flaws and call into question their talent."[31] With the second group, which received praise for their effort, 90 percent of the students desired a challenging new task from which they could grow and learn.[32] It's important not just to praise your team but also to praise them specifically in diversity and inclusion efforts.

11. Be all in. What would it look like for you to be fully invested in diversity and inclusion efforts? What behavior would you model, and how would others know this is more to you than just a statement? I remember going to speak for one of my clients, Burns & McDonnell, for the kickoff of their diversity month, and they had just brought in a new CEO. The CEO introduced the day as normal, but then he did something I've rarely seen any other CEO or executive leaders do, beyond the vice president of diversity and inclusion. He sat down and stayed the entire day. He even attended lunch with me and the Diversity and Inclusion committee. His presence communicated to me and to his team that he was all in. While no one leader is perfect, his presence made a powerful statement. Take an active role in diversity and inclusion efforts as a leader, not as a passive presence. Join an employee resource group, attend meaningful functions, and mentor employees from underrepresented groups. Your presence communicates more than you know. Another way to be all in is to leverage organizations like SHRM (Society for Human Resource Management) to better understand the organizational landscape of diversity and inclusion. They have data, benchmarks, and useful tools to help leaders and organizations.

12. Believe in your people. Intentionally Inclusive Leaders believe that no matter the background of their people, they can grow, develop, and have meaningful progress in diversity and inclusion. In a 1968 study by Rosenthal and Jacobson, what teachers in the study thought of their students came true. The teachers were given a list of the most gifted children in their class, and at the end of the school year, the students on that list had performed the best. It is important to note that the list was chosen at random.

If the teacher thought a particular student was gifted, they treated that child differently from the others. For example, when a student on the gifted list wasn't performing well, the teacher felt that the student just wasn't motivated enough, and therefore the teacher changed her approach. But for the students not on the list, the teachers assumed those students didn't perform well because they lacked the ability, and that factor was unchangeable.[33] How you see your people has an impact on how you lead them, even subconsciously. Dweck states, "The great teachers believe in the growth of the intellect and talent, and they are fascinated with the process of learning."[34]

13. Amplify others. IILs don't ignore or minimize marginalized or underrepresented groups; on the contrary, they magnify the voices of these groups by intentionally seeking their feedback and following up. They empower all team members to contribute and make decisions. They share the successes of their team with other key leaders and create spaces for the team members to have visibility. Take the advice of Elizabeth McKee, executive director of Leadership Charlotte, when she says leaders need to be able to see "who's not in the room and whose voice is not here."[35] Part of amplifying is creating space for those who are not in the room.

14. Set high standards. Dweck states, "Great teachers set high standards for all their students, not just the ones who are already achieving."[36] This also applies to great leaders. On your team and in your company, set and communicate high standards for diversity and inclusion—one where discrimination will not be tolerated and systems are open to be improved, fixed, or deconstructed. At the same time, it is important to encourage personal risk-taking (being comfortable with the uncomfortable) while withholding fast judgment.

15. Share the credit. Sharing the credit when progress is made in diversity and inclusion creates a shared success for your team. When everyone is held accountable, everyone can also be appreciated and inspired by the amazing wins of the organization or team.

Being an Intentionally Inclusive Leader is important as you shape the culture of your organization and team. These are just a few ways you can step up more as a leader and have a true impact. What is one thing on this list that you can commit to over the next thirty to sixty days? You can't do everything at once, but you can dig deep into one area and make progress as an Intentionally Inclusive Leader.

ACTION FORWARD

1. Which one of the fifteen tips will you commit to incorporating as an Intentionally Inclusive Leader?

2. Consider asking members of your team how you can better help them bring their true and best selves to work.

3. Do you find the business case or the humanity case more compelling? Why?

ACKNOWLEDGMENTS

I first want to say thank you to my mom-e! You have been a true diversity and inclusion hero in my life, and I am grateful (even when you made me do the dishes).

Thank you to my Work Meaningful team. Dari, I could not have done this without you. You have been a true work partner as you allowed me to focus on writing this book while you took care of the day-to-day business needs. You are *so* valuable. Paa, thank you for representing us well in Ghana and for continuing to help our company grow.

Thank you to Jackie Hrabowski for opening me up to the diversity and inclusion world by allowing me to get involved with our Employee Resource Group.

A special thank-you to a continued mentor, Forest Harper, who has constantly challenged me and helped shape how I approach diversity and inclusion. We've come a long way, Forest (from Morgan State University, Pfizer, and INROADS). I am so thankful for how you formally and informally have prepared me for this moment and moments to come.

Thank you, Susan Johnson, for giving a name to the work I do. I was inspired when you called me an "on-ramper." Your words have helped me see my value in helping people get onto the highway of diversity and inclusion. Your heartfelt work continues to inspire me.

A special thank-you to all my clients who have invited me to share my message to tens of thousands of your employees, teams, staff, and students. To name a few, thank you to Susan Johnson (the Hartford), Kim Davis (NFP), Lisa Harris (Toyota), O. J. Robertson

(Mercedes-Benz), Debra Chew (NIH), Sandra Scott (University of Wisconsin-Stout), Dan Sullivan and Babs Smith (the Strategic Coach), Kasi Allen and Katherine Gandee (the Ford Family Foundation), and the countless corporations, colleges, and faith communities that have been instrumental in my journey. While I shared with you, I was learning from you at the same time.

I am so grateful for all those who carved out their time for me to interview for this project. While some of you are in this book, others of you shaped how I wrote this book and the information I included. Thank you to Kim Davis, Raven Solomon, Daniel Fajardo, Elizabeth McKee, James Robilotta and Tina Vansteenbergen Robilotta, Jeremy Poincenot, Matt Aghedo, Otis Pickett, Melody Gross, Jess Pettitt, and Valerie Jones-Williams.

Thank you to those who helped me, challenged me, and gave me space to write and create. Thank you to my precious kiddos for sacrificing a few of our backyard soccer games and tickle challenges so Dad-e could write. Thank you to Jon Clemons, Aprill Ergas, Ken Patterson, Nunca, Darryl Bellamy, Ariel Perry, and my mastermind group (Marcey Rader, Stan Phelps, David Rendall, Jeff Nischwitz, and Kevin Snyder). Thank you to Chris West, Ruchira Disgupta, and the whole Video Narrative team for working with me to further develop my brand, my website, and video!

I would like to thank my editor, Darcie Clemen Robertson. Your patience and professionalism are amazing. Thanks for organizing the process and enduring my "I need two more days" emails. Thank you to my designer, U.T. Designs. Thank you to my creative team who worked on all the amazing graphics.

Last but not least, thank you to YOU for investing in this book and reading it. I hope that we continue to create an amazing world for today and tomorrow with the Inclusive Mindset!

ADDITIONAL RESOURCES

Visit the resources section of theinclusivemindset.com for the following:

1. The Inclusive Mindset Plan (Template)
2. Common diversity and inclusion terminology
3. Recommended books, articles, and videos
4. Ways to help your organization live out these values
5. Other valuable resources to help you cultivate diversity and inclusion every day in your life and your organization

NOTES

Chapter 1: *What Type of Hugger Are You?*

1. Kay Vandette, "The Healing Power of a Hug Is Real, New Study Reveals," Earth. com, October 3, 2018, https://www.earth.com/news/hug-healing-power/.
2. "The Power of Hugs and How They Affect Our Daily Health," *SCL Health* (blog), July 2019, https://www.sclhealth.org/blog/2019/07/the-power-of-hugs-and-how -they-affect-our-daily-health/.
3. Author interview with Valerie Jones-Williams via phone on November 10, 2020.
4. Robin Ely and David Thomas, "Getting Serious about Diversity: Enough Already with the Business Case," *Harvard Business Review*, November–December 2020, https://hbr.org/2020/11/getting-serious-about-diversity-enough-already-with -the-business-case.
5. "(1857) Frederick Douglass, 'If There Is No Struggle, There Is No Progress,'" BlackPast, January 25, 2007, https://www.blackpast.org/african-american-history /1857-frederick-douglass-if-there-no-struggle-there-no-progress/.

Chapter 2: *The Secret Revealed*

1. Dictionary.com, s.v. "cultivate," accessed January 10, 2021, https://www.dictionary .com/browse/cultivate.
2. J. D. Meier, "What Is Mindset?," Sources of Insight, http://sourcesofinsight.com /what-is-mindset/.
3. Carol S. Dweck, *Mindset: The New Psychology of Success* (New York: Ballantine Books, 2016), 16, emphasis in original.
4. Dweck, 28.
5. Dweck, 98.
6. Dweck, 21.
7. Dweck, 50.
8. Dweck, 22.
9. Dweck, 7.
10. Dweck, 48, emphasis in original.
11. Dweck, 42.
12. Dweck, 42.
13. Dweck, 25.
14. Dweck, 75–76.
15. Dweck, 191.
16. Dweck, 36.
17. Dweck, 109.

Chapter 3: *Diversity Redefined*

1. Merriam-Webster, s.v. "diversity," accessed January 10, 2021, https://www.merriam-webster.com/dictionary/diversity.
2. Wikipedia, s.v. "business case," accessed January 10, 2021, https://en.wikipedia.org/wiki/Business_case.
3. Vivian Hunt et al., *Delivering Through Diversity* (Denver: McKinsey & Company, 2018), https://www.mckinsey.com/~/media/mckinsey/business%20functions/organization/our%20insights/delivering%20through%20diversity/delivering-through-diversity_full-report.ashx.
4. Kevin Dolan et al., "Diversity Still Matters," *McKinsey Quarterly*, May 19, 2020, https://www.mckinsey.com/featured-insights/diversity-and-inclusion/diversity-still-matters.
5. "Focusing on What Works for Workplace Diversity," McKinsey & Company, April 7, 2017, https://www.mckinsey.com/featured-insights/gender-equality/focusing-on-what-works-for-workplace-diversity.
6. Juliet Bourke, "The Six Signature Traits of Inclusive Leadership," Deloitte Insights, April 14, 2016, https://www2.deloitte.com/us/en/insights/topics/talent/six-signature-traits-of-inclusive-leadership.html.
7. Jeanine Prime and Corinne A. Moss-Racusin, *Engaging Men in Gender Initiatives: What Change Agents Need to Know* (n.p.: Catalyst, 2009), http://www.catalyst.org/knowledge/engaging-men-gender-initiatives-what-change-agents-need-know, quoted in Bourke, "Six Signature Traits."
8. Thomas H. Davenport and Brook Manville, *Judgment Calls: Twelve Stories of Big Decisions and the Teams That Got Them Right* (Boston: Harvard Business School Publishing, 2012), quoted in Bourke, "Six Signature Traits."

Chapter 4: *Defining the Inclusive Mindset*

1. Teresa Amabile and Steven Kramer, *The Progress Principle: Using Small Wins to Ignite Joy, Engagement, and Creativity at Work* (Boston: Harvard Business School Publishing, 2011), 77.
2. Carol S. Dweck, *Mindset: The New Psychology of Success* (New York: Ballantine Books, 2016), 224.

Chapter 5: *Circles of Grace*

1. Lisa M. Osbeck, Fathali M. Moghaddam, and Stephanie Perreault, "Similarity and Attraction among Majority and Minority Groups in a Multicultural Context," *International Journal of Intercultural Relations* 21, no. 1 (1997), http://fathalimoghaddam.com/wp-content/uploads/2013/10/1256666068.pdf, 114.
2. University of Glasgow, "Remembering the Future: Our Brain Saves Energy by Predicting What It Will See," Medical XPress, March 24, 2010, https://medicalxpress.com/news/2010-03-future-brain-energy.html.
3. Author interview with James Robilotta via Zoom on October 19, 2020.
4. Vernā Myers, "How to Overcome Our Biases? Walk Boldly toward Them," TED Talk, November 2014, https://www.ted.com/talks/verna_myers_how_to_overcome_our_biases_walk_boldly_toward_them.

5. Alice Boyes, "6 Ways to Overcome Your Biases for Good," *Psychology Today*, August 20, 2015, https://www.psychologytoday.com/intl/blog/in-practice /201508/6-ways-overcome-your-biases-good.

6. A. G. Greenwald and M. R. Banaji, "Implicit social cognition: attitudes, self-esteem, and stereotypes," *Psychological Review* 102, no. 1 (1995): 4, and A. G. Greenwald and L. H. Krieger, "Implicit bias: Scientific foundations," *California Law Review* 94, no. 4 (2006): 945–967, quoted in Charlotte Ruhl, "Implicit or Unconscious Bias," Simply Psychology, July 1, 2020, https://www.simply psychology.org/implicit-bias.html.

7. Dina Gerdeman, "Minorities Who 'Whiten' Job Resumes Get More Interviews," Working Knowledge, Harvard Business School, May 17, 2017, https://hbswk .hbs.edu/item/minorities-who-whiten-job-resumes-get-more-interviews.

8. Gerdeman, "Minorities Who 'Whiten' Job Resumes Get More Interviews."

9. Johns Hopkins University, "Babies' Random Choices Become Their Preferences," Science Daily, October 2, 2020, www.sciencedaily.com/releases/2020/10/20100209 1027.htm.

Chapter 6: *Welcoming vs. Inviting*

1. Christine W. Li, "Diversity without Inclusion Is Exclusion," DIA Global Forum, January 2018, https://globalforum.diaglobal.org/issue/january-2018/diversity -without-inclusion-is-exclusion/.

2. Author interview with Daniel Fajardo via Zoom on October 29, 2020.

3. Steven Huang, "Why Does Belonging Matter at Work?," *The SHRM Blog*, July 3, 2020, https://blog.shrm.org/blog/why-does-belonging-matter-at-work#:~:text =Belonging%20is%20defined%20as%20the,a%20diverse%20and%20inclusive% 20place.

4. Karyn Hall, "Create a Sense of Belonging," *Psychology Today*, March 24, 2014, https://www.psychologytoday.com/us/blog/pieces-mind/201403/create-sense -belonging.

5. Author interview with Jess Pettitt via Zoom on October 31, 2020.

Chapter 7: *Stupid Stuff Smart People Say*

1. Andrew Limbong, "Microaggressions Are a Big Deal: How to Talk Them Out and When to Walk Away," NPR, June 9, 2020, https://www.npr.org/2020 /06/08/872371063/microaggressions-are-a-big-deal-how-to-talk-them-out-and -when-to-walk-away.

2. Jessica Caporuscio, "What to Know about Microaggressions in the Workplace," Medical News Today, July 22, 2020, https://www.medicalnewstoday.com/articles /microaggressions-in-the-workplace#what-they-are.

3. Author interview with Jeremy Poincenot via Zoom on October 15, 2020.

Chapter 8: *The Kid on the Plane Who Wouldn't Shut Up*

1. George Loewenstein, "The Psychology of Curiosity: A Review and Reinterpretation," *Psychological Bulletin* 116, no. 1 (1994):75–98, quoted in Celeste Kidd and

Benjamin Y. Hayden, "The Psychology and Neuroscience of Curiosity," *Neuron* 88, no. 3 (November 2015): 449–60.

2. M. J. Kang et al., "The Wick in the Candle of Learning: Epistemic Curiosity Activates Reward Circuitry and Enhances Memory," *Psychological Science* 20, no. 8 (August 2009): 963–73.

3. Reniqua Allen, "The Story We Tell about Millennials and Who We Leave Out," TED Salon, January 2019, https://www.ted.com/talks/reniqua_allen_the_story_we_tell_about_millennials_and_who_we_leave_out?language=en.

4. "Active Listening Skills: Definitions and Examples," Career Guide, Indeed, February 8, 2021, https://www.indeed.com/career-advice/career-development/active-listening-skills.

5. Jack Zenger and Joseph Folkman, "What Great Listeners Actually Do," *Harvard Business Review*, July 14, 2016, https://hbr.org/2016/07/what-great-listeners-actually-do.

6. Bob Sullivan and Hugh Thompson, "Now Hear This! Most People Stink at Listening," *Scientific American*, May 3, 2013, https://www.scientificamerican.com/article/plateau-effect-digital-gadget-distraction-attention/.

7. Diana I. Tamir and Jason P. Mitchell, "Disclosing Information about the Self Is Intrinsically Rewarding," *Proceedings of the National Academy of Sciences of the United States of America* 109, no. 21 (May 2012): 8038–43.

8. Alison Wood Brooks and Leslie K. John, "The Surprising Power of Questions," *Harvard Business Review*, May–June 2018, https://hbr.org/2018/05/the-surprising-power-of-questions.

9. Brooks and John, "Surprising Power of Questions."

Chapter 9: *Discovering Dialogue and Exercising Empathy*

1. William Isaacs, *Dialogue and the Art of Thinking Together* (New York: Random House, 1999), 19.

2. Isaacs, 9.

3. Isaacs, 9.

4. Issacs, 5.

5. Isaacs, 83–176.

6. Ben Montgomery, Kelley Benham French, and Thomas French, "21 Americans with Opposing Views on Guns Sat Down to Talk to Each Other. Here's What They Discovered," Time.com, June 28, 2018, https://time.com/longform/both-sides-gun-control/.

7. Frank J. Lambrechts et al., "Learning to Help through Humble Inquiry and Implications for Management Research, Practice, and Education: An Interview with Edgar H. Schein," *Academy of Management Learning and Education* 10, no. 1 (March 2011): 131–47.

8. Andrea Brandt, "Learn Empathy in Just 5 Steps," *Psychology Today*, September 6, 2018, https://www.psychologytoday.com/us/blog/mindful-anger/201809/learn-empathy-in-just-5-steps.

9. Sara Konrath, "Speaking of Psychology: The Decline of Empathy and the Rise of Narcissism," American Psychological Association, https://www.apa.org/research/action/speaking-of-psychology/empathy-narcissism.

10. Justin Bariso, "There Are Actually 3 Types of Empathy. Here's How They Differ—and How You Can Develop Them All," Inc., September 19, 2018, https://www.inc.com/justin-bariso/there-are-actually-3-types-of-empathy-heres-how-they-differ-and-how-you-can-develop-them-all.html.

11. S. H. Konrath, E. H. O'Brien, and C. Hsing, "Changes in Dispositional Empathy in American College Students over Time: A Meta-Analysis," Personality and Social Psychology Review 15, no. 2 (May 2011), https://journals.sagepub.com/doi/abs/10.1177/1088868310377395.

12. Konrath, O'Brien, and Hsing, "Changes in Dispositional Empathy."

13. American Psychological Association, "Empathy Often Avoided Because of Mental Effort," Science Daily, April 22, 2019, https://www.sciencedaily.com/releases/2019/04/190422090847.htm.

14. Neel Burton, "Empathy vs. Sympathy," Psychology Today, updated April 27, 2020, https://www.psychologytoday.com/us/blog/hide-and-seek/201505/empathy-vs-sympathy.

15. Adam Waytz, "The Limits of Empathy," Harvard Business Review, January–February 2016, https://hbr.org/2016/01/the-limits-of-empathy.

16. Author interview with Matt Aghedo via Zoom on October 27, 2020.

Chapter 10: The Right-Hand Paradigm

1. Roger Dobson, "The Loneliness of the Left-Handed Surgeon," BMJ 330, no. 10 (December 2004).

2. Sian Ferguson, "Privilege 101: A Quick and Dirty Guide," Everyday Feminism, September 29, 2014, https://everydayfeminism.com/2014/09/what-is-privilege/.

3. Maisha Z. Johnson, "What Privilege Really Means (and Doesn't Mean)—to Clear Up Your Doubts Once and for All," Everyday Feminism, July 21, 2015, https://everydayfeminism.com/2015/07/what-privilege-really-means/.

4. Johnson, "What Privilege Really Means."

5. Author interview with Melody Gross via Zoom on October 20, 2020.

6. Allan G. Johnson, Privilege, Power, and Difference (New York: McGraw-Hill Education, 2006), 38–39.

7. Johnson, Privilege, Power, and Difference, 127.

Chapter 11: The Moving Walkway

1. Author interview with Otis Pickett via Zoom on October 15, 2020.

2. Robert Livingston, "How to Promote Racial Equity in the Workplace," Harvard Business Review, September–October 2020, https://hbr.org/2020/09/how-to-promote-racial-equity-in-the-workplace.

3. Livingston, "How to Promote Racial Equity in the Workplace."

4. Author interview with Raven Solomon via Zoom on October 26, 2020.

5. Author interview with Raven Solomon via Zoom on October 26, 2020.

6. Livingston, "How to Promote Racial Equity in the Workplace."
7. Ibram X. Kendi, *How to Be an Anti-Racist* (New York: Random House, 2019), 10.

Chapter 12: *The Glass Half . . .*

1. Alison Pearce Stevens, "Learning Rewires the Brain," Science News for Students, September 2, 2014, https://www.sciencenewsforstudents.org/article /learning-rewires-brain.
2. Rick Hanson, "Just One Thing: Pay Attention!," *Greater Good Magazine*, October 5, 2015, https://greatergood.berkeley.edu/article/item/just_one_thing_pay _attention.
3. P. Lally et al., "How Are Habits Formed: Modelling Habit Formation in the Real World," *European Journal of Social Psychology* 40, no. 6 (October 2010): 998–1009, https://doi.org/10.1002/ejsp.674.
4. Sarah Milne, Sheina Orbell, and Paschal Sheeran, "Combining Motivational and Volitional Interventions to Promote Exercise Participation: Protection Motivation Theory and Implementation Intentions," *British Journal of Health Psychology* 7, pt. 2 (May 2002): 163–84.

Appendix: *How to Be an Intentionally Inclusive Leader*

1. Author interview with Elizabeth McKee via Zoom on October 19, 2020.
2. Robert Livingston, "How to Promote Racial Equity in the Workplace," *Harvard Business Review*, September–October 2020, https://hbr.org/2020/09/how-to -promote-racial-equity-in-the-workplace.
3. Robin J. Ely and David A. Thomas, "Getting Serious about Diversity: Enough Already with the Business Case," *Harvard Business Review*, November– December 2020, https://hbr.org/2020/11/getting-serious-about-diversity -enough-already-with-the-business-case.
4. Michael Slepian, "Are Your D&I Efforts Helping Employees Feel Like They Belong?" *Harvard Business Review*, August 19, 2020, https://hbr.org/2020/08 /are-your-di-efforts-helping-employees-feel-like-they-belong.
5. Slepian, "Are Your D&I Efforts Helping Employees."
6. Ely and Thomas, "Getting Serious about Diversity."
7. "The Five Disciplines of Inclusive Leaders," Korn Ferry, https://infokf.kornferry .com/inclusive-leader-lu.html.
8. Juliet Bourke, "The Six Signature Traits of Inclusive Leadership," Deloitte Insights, April 14, 2016, https://www2.deloitte.com/us/en/insights/topics/talent/six -signature-traits-of-inclusive-leadership.html.
9. Vivian Hunt et al., *Delivering through Diversity* (Denver: McKinsey & Company, 2018), https://www.mckinsey.com/~/media/mckinsey/business%20functions /organization/our%20insights/delivering%20through%20diversity/delivering -through-diversity_full-report.ashx, 12.
10. Hunt et al., *Delivering through Diversity*, 4.
11. Ely and Thomas, "Getting Serious about Diversity."
12. Ely and Thomas, "Getting Serious about Diversity."

13. Sarah Kaplan, "Why the 'Business Case' for Diversity Isn't Working," *Fast Company*, February 12, 2020, https://www.fastcompany.com/90462867/why-the-business-case-for-diversity-isnt-working.
14. Ely and Thomas, "Getting Serious about Diversity."
15. Ely and Thomas, "Getting Serious about Diversity."
16. Kaplan, "Why the 'Business Case' for Diversity Isn't Working."
17. Brian Ramírez and Juan María Gómez, "The People Who Bought a Gym and Tried to Change a City," BBC Reel (video), January 25, 2021, https://www.bbc.com/reel/video/p094qhsz/the-people-who-bought-a-gym-and-tried-to-change-a-city.
18. Jeffrey Hiatt, *ADKAR: A Model for Change in Business, Government and Our Community* (Loveland, CO: Prosci Learning Center Publications, 2006).
19. "What Is the ADKAR Model?," Prosci, https://www.prosci.com/adkar/adkar-model.
20. Jennifer Brown, *How to Be an Inclusive Leader: Your Role in Creating Cultures of Belonging Where Everyone Can Thrive* (Oakland, CA: Berrett-Koehler, 2019), 107.
21. Charlotte Sweeney and Fleur Bothwick, *Inclusive Leadership* (UK: Pearson Education Limited, 2016), 224.
22. Author interview with Kim Davis via Zoom on October 20, 2020.
23. Bernadette Dillon and Juliet Bourke, *The Six Signature Traits of Inclusive Leadership* (UK: Deloitte University Press, 2016), https://www2.deloitte.com/content/dam/Deloitte/au/Documents/human-capital/deloitte-au-hc-six-signature-traits-inclusive-leadership-020516.pdf.
24. "Empathy Stats and Facts for Business," Brand Genetics, October 10, 2019, https://brandgenetics.com/empathy-statistics-for-business/.
25. Ely and Thomas, "Getting Serious about Diversity."
26. John Scorza, "Accelerate Positive Change: A Q&A with Ben Hasan," *HR Magazine*, August 20, 2020, https://www.shrm.org/hr-today/news/hr-magazine/fall2020/pages/accelerate-positive-change-ben-hasan-interview.aspx.
27. Ely and Thomas, "Getting Serious about Diversity."
28. Author interview with Daniel Fajardo via Zoom on October 29, 2020.
29. Livingston, "How to Promote Racial Equity in the Workplace," 8–9.
30. David Pedulla, "Diversity and Inclusion Efforts That Really Work," *Harvard Business Review*, May 12, 2020, https://hbr.org/2020/05/diversity-and-inclusion-efforts-that-really-work.
31. Carol S. Dweck, *Mindset: The New Psychology of Success* (New York: Ballantine Books, 2016), 72.
32. Dweck, 71–72.
33. Robert Rosenthal and Lenore Jacobson, *Pygmalion in the Classroom* (Norwalk, CT: Crown House, 1992), chap. 7.
34. Dweck, *Mindset*, 197.
35. Author interview with Elizabeth McKee via Zoom on October 19, 2020.
36. Dweck, *Mindset*, 200.

THE INCLUSIVE MINDSET ORGANIZATION™

TheInclusiveMindsetOrg.com

I have had the privilege of working with some amazing organizations and teams (virtually and in person) to really move the needle in diversity and inclusion. I have found a process that has worked and has helped numerous organizations move forward by inspiring their employees, teams, and leaders toward a more Inclusive Mindset. If you are interested in helping your organization become an Inclusive Mindset Organization, visit us at the website above.

What is our approach? We work with you to create a customized plan to bring along the most people possible focusing on progress, not perfection. We are a great starting or restarting point for organizations that are serious about how to move forward in being more diverse and inclusive. We have worked with organizations from the Fortune 50, universities, nonprofits, foundations, and faith communities.

Some of the items that are available in our customized approach are

- Pre-test/post-test surveys (to measure impact)
- Focus groups
- Trainings/workshops
- Keynote presentations
- Additional resources to go deeper
- Advisement sessions for leaders focused on change management for diversity and inclusion

WAYS WE HAVE WORKED WITH CLIENTS

There is no cookie-cutter approach to diversity and inclusion within your organization. Here are some ways I have partnered with organizations:

- The Inclusive Mindset Organization process: agreement, assessment, alignment, and advancement with advisement sessions for leaders and change makers
- Using this book as a guide and creating a workshop plan based on each chapter
- Using the seven mini-episodes of *Everyday Diversity Series* as a guide and creating a workshop plan based on them
- Customized presentations for conferences

If you feel your organization may benefit

from this approach, visit with us at

TheInclusiveMindsetOrg.com

SHARE YOUR THOUGHTS

The biggest thank-you one can give is leaving an honest review. It is also the best way for others to learn and share the Inclusive Mindset vision with others. Please consider going to Amazon or wherever you purchased this book and sharing your perspective. Thank you for helping to spread the message of *The Inclusive Mindset* with others.

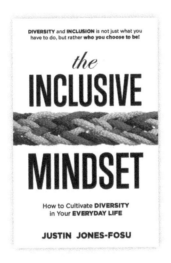

You are appreciated! Thank you in advance. Also, if you would like to share how this book impacted you, consider emailing me directly at engage@workmeaningful.com.

ALSO BY JUSTIN

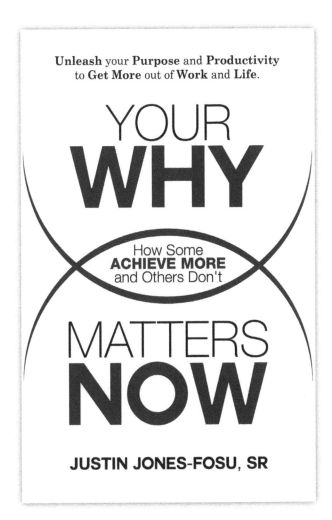

Unleash your **Purpose** and **Productivity**
to **Get More** out of **Work** and **Life**.

YOUR
WHY

How Some
ACHIEVE MORE
and Others Don't

MATTERS
NOW

JUSTIN JONES-FOSU, SR

yourwhymattersnow.com